100 Treasures & Curiosities

From the collection of Carisbrooke Castle Museum

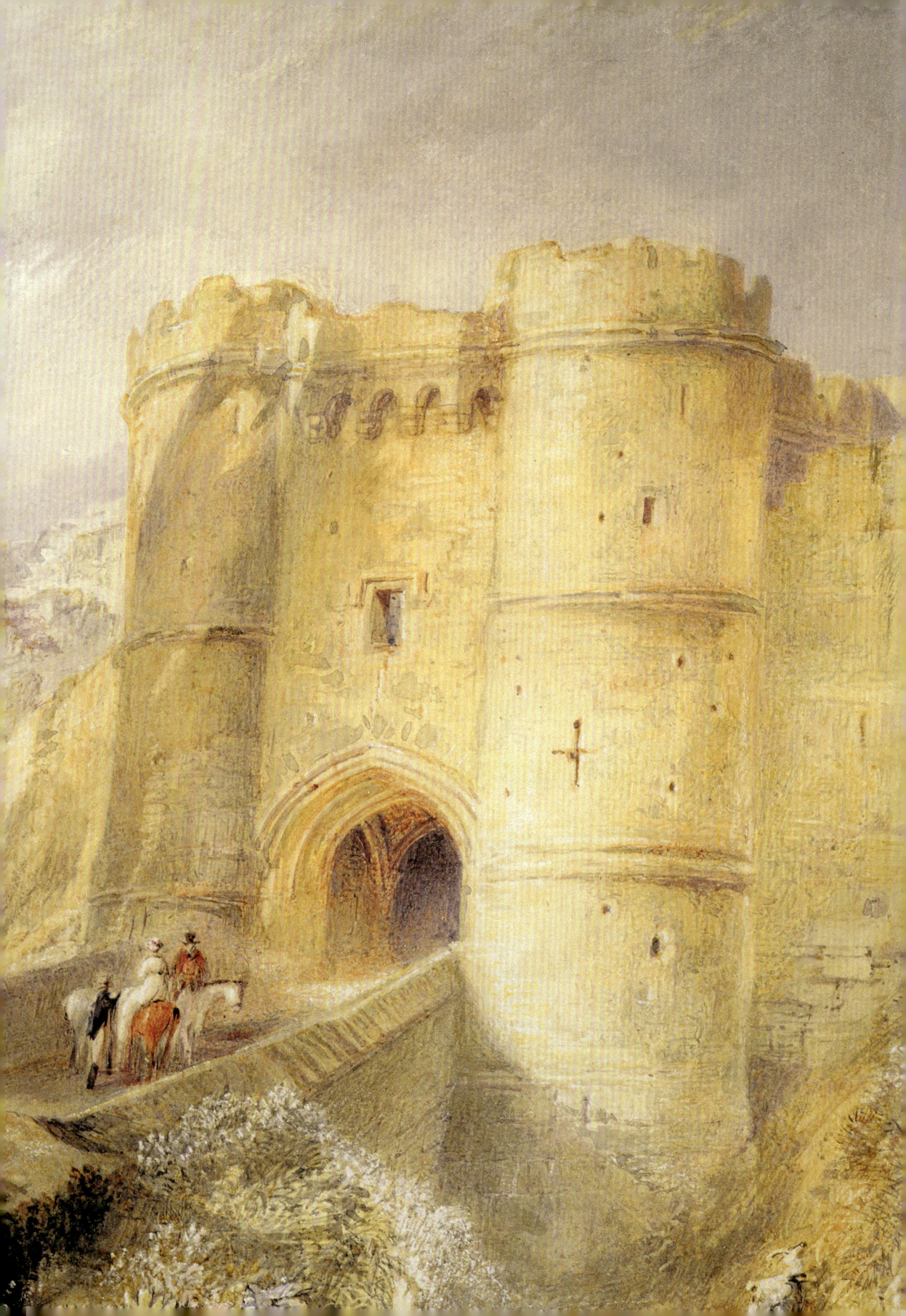

100 Treasures & Curiosities

From the collection of Carisbrooke Castle Museum

Dr. Rachel Tait

Kate Tiley

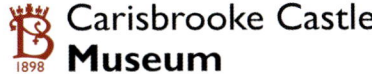
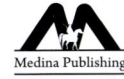

Published in collaboration with Medina Publishing
50 High Street, Cowes
PO31 7RR United Kingdom
www.medinapublishing.com

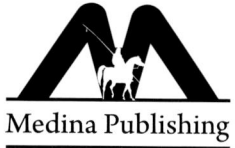

The moral right of the authors has been asserted. All rights reserved.
No part of this publication may be reproduced, stored in a retrieval system or transmitted in any form or by any means, whether electronic or mechanical, including photocopying, recording or otherwise without the prior permission in writing of the publisher.

All text and images copyright © Carisbrooke Castle Museum 2023

ISBN - 978-1-911487-97-5

A CIP catalogue record for this book is available from the British Library.

Printed in Wales by Gomer Press Ltd on FSC-certified paper.

Contents

Acknowledgments		8
Foreword		10
Introduction		12
100 Treasures & Curiosities		26
1.	Ceremonial key	27
2.	Palaeolithic hand axes	28
3.	Bronze Age flanged axe	29
4.	Bronze Age collared urn	30
5.	Wolf claw necklace	31
6.	Roman Vectis Ware pot	32
7.	Stone Janus head	34
8.	Anglo-Saxon urn	35
9.	Anglo-Saxon keystone brooches	36
10.	Anglo-Saxon bronze disc brooches	37
11.	Anglo-Saxon glass armlet	38
12.	Chevron glass bead	39
13.	Walrus ivory tableman	40
14.	Charter of Nicholas le Sumpter	42
15.	Newtown mace	43
16.	Letter written in code by Charles I	44
17.	Civil War news sheet	46
18.	Charles I's linen nightcap	47
19.	Locket containing hair of Charles I	48
20.	The Royal Prisoners by C.W. Cope, 1855	50
21.	Ring containing a fragment of Princess Elizabeth's dress	52
22.	Maquette for a monument to Princess Elizabeth	53
23.	Locks of Princess Elizabeth's hair	54
24.	Alabaster statue of Virgin and child	56
25.	Decorated tile from the old St Thomas's Church	57
26.	Elizabethan communion cup	58
27.	Bible and prayer book	59
28.	Gold posy ring	60
29.	Georgian wedding waistcoat	61
30.	St Dominic's Vestment	62
31.	Walter Caws' sermon timer	64

32.	Tudor hornbook	65
33.	Blue Jenny	66
34.	Embroidered sampler	68
35.	Nunn's lace factory pattern book	69
36.	John Buncombe's paint box	70
37.	Newport High Street by John Nixon	72
38.	Newport trade tokens	74
39.	Leather hat found at the Green Dragon Inn	75
40.	Beer firkin	76
41.	Worker's smock	77
42.	Anti-poaching spring gun	78
43.	Smuggling 'peep tub'	79
44.	Pewter tankard	80
45.	Churchwarden's clay pipe, made by Robert Cole	81
46.	Ale muller	82
47.	Tin of Mew's Ale	83
48.	Shipwreck logbook	84
49.	Fragment of the wreck of the Royal George	86
50.	Ship's medicine chest	88
51.	Figurehead of the Auguste of Brake	90
52.	Sand picture of the wrecked Perlen by Charles Plumley	92
53.	Ship's biscuit from the wreck of the Irex	93
54.	Coastguard helmet	94
55.	Frank Salter's RNLI medal	95
56.	Carisbrooke Castle by J. M. W. Turner, 1828	96
57.	Alfred, Lord Tennyson: 'The Dirty Monk' by Julia Margaret Cameron, 1865	98
58.	Alfred, Lord Tennyson's pipe rack	100
59.	Worsley family seal	101
60.	Charles 'Pound Hammer' Kingswell	102
61.	Ambrotype of Mary Merwood	104
62.	Watercolour of Pan Down by Fanny Minns	105
63.	Hairpiece and crocheted bonnet	106
64.	Emma Denett's botanical album	108
65.	Study of bird eggs by Harriet Darwin Fox, 1839	110
66.	Eel pass tile	111
67.	Horatio Dennett's model steam engine	112
68.	East Cowes Castle Clock	114
69.	'Sunbeam' lightbulb	115
70.	Wooden water mains pipe	116
71.	Nurse Wilson's typhoid epidemic medal	117

72.	George Brannon artist's proof	118
73.	Professor John Milne's laboratory at Shide Hill House	120
74.	Yachting bodice	122
75.	Redfern and Sons 'tailor-made' style jacket	123
76.	Shanklin beach by Alfred Harcourt, 1874	124
77.	Empress Eugénie's bathing shoes	126
78.	Stereoscopic photograph of the Needles	127
79.	Princess Beatrice's drawers	128
80.	Clockwork swimming doll	129
81.	Doll's house	130
82.	Inuit doll made in Lapland	132
83.	Beads from Ur	133
84.	Somerset John Gough-Calthorpe's Dragoon Guards Helmet	134
85.	Japanese Aikuchi	136
86.	Miniature portraits of Prince Henry and Princess Beatrice	138
87.	Prince Henry's Isle of Wight Rifles sword	140
88.	George V's Isle of Wight Rifles jacket	142
89.	Frederick Nobbs' Boer War pipe	144
90.	World War One pith helmet	145
91.	Private Archibald Warren's World War One memorial plaque	146
92.	Lieut. Reginald Denham's World War One compass	148
93.	Terracotta caricature of Hitler	150
94.	World War Two shrapnel	152
95.	Shipyard clog	153
96.	Pair of ladies' python skin shoes	154
97.	Isle of Wight Handcraft Pottery	156
98.	Ceramic vessel	157
99.	Love Wins t-shirt	158
100.	Home-made scrubs	159

Further Reading & Authors   160

Acknowledgments

This book's creation was motivated by a desire to mark the Museum's 125th anniversary with a celebration of its diverse and fascinating collections. This would not have been possible without the generosity of a number of supporters: the Friends of Carisbrooke Castle Museum, the Herepath Shenton Trust and the Isle of Wight AONB. We would like to thank them all for helping make this idea a reality. We would also like to thank all the individuals and businesses who have supported the project by sponsoring one of the artefacts – we hope you enjoy discovering more about these treasures and curiosities.

Our understanding of these artefacts depends on the work of a number of earlier Museum Curators and other researchers. In particular, we have drawn extensively on the research of Rosemary Cooper (former Curator and current Trustee) and Paul Bingham in our discussion of the museum's early history. Primary research undertaken by Christina Tiley has helped increase our understanding of the local significance of several objects and both Rosemary and Christina provided valuable feedback on drafts of the text. We have also appreciated the assistance of the Isle of Wight Council's Heritage Service and Archaeology and Historic Environment Service in providing information about a number of artefacts. Tracy Borman generously supplied a lively foreword, and the photographs which bring the objects to life and reveal their beauty and interest were taken by David Whistance. We are grateful to him for the time he gave to the project and for a donation from Phoebe Jane Smith (née Stark) whose gift in memory of the Stark family also contributed to this. Finally, we would like to thank all the volunteers who have supported the project in various ways, from helping us retrieve objects from stores to locating information in the museum library, and who are vital to the day-to-day running of the museum.

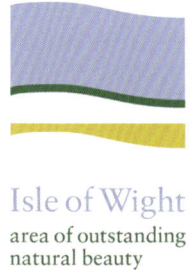

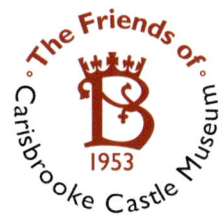

Herapath Shenton

Foreword

One of my most memorable experiences during the many years I have worked for Historic Royal Palaces was retracing the steps of Charles I, the captive king who made a daring escape from Hampton Court. In 1646, he had been put under house arrest by the orders of his nemesis, Oliver Cromwell, as civil war raged across the kingdom. With the help of his accomplices, Charles was spirited away to the Isle of Wight and placed under the care of its Governor, Colonel Robert Hammond, who was believed to be sympathetic to the Royalist cause. Sadly, for the beleaguered king, he proved anything but. Charles was held captive at the ancient fortress of Carisbrooke Castle. He tried to escape, but failed to do so. After spending a year on the Island, the king was taken back to London where he was tried and executed in January 1649.

After following in the footsteps of the ill-fated king, I was only able to go as far as the banks of the Thames next to Hampton Court. Sadly, there was no waiting barge to carry me to the beautiful Isle of Wight, a place very close to my heart. I first discovered the Island whilst working for English Heritage in the early 2000s. I have been back many times during the intervening years: speaking at the annual literary festival, holidaying with my family and cycling around its stunning and hilly coastline. I'm now proud to be a patron of the Vectis Archaeological Trust.

The story of Charles I's captivity is just one of many from the Island's history in general, and Carisbrooke Castle Museum in particular, that are explored in this wonderful book. A lock of his hair, donated to the museum by Queen Victoria (another devotee of the Island, whose daughter Beatrice founded the museum) is featured, as are ninety-nine further treasures. They include a ring containing a piece of the dress that Charles's daughter Elizabeth died in, George V's Isle of Wight Rifles uniform jacket and an exquisite Anglo-Saxon gold and garnet brooch. As well as being objects of interest and beauty, each one has a fascinating tale to tell. I hope you will enjoy discovering their stories as much as I did.

Tracy Borman

Introduction

> *"It is my earnest hope and desire that with the help and co-operation of others I may be able to form a full collection of objects of historical interest connected with the Island, so that this memorial gatehouse may become a museum worthy of such an interesting castle."*
>
> *- HRH Princess Beatrice of Battenberg*

On August 11th, 1898, Princess Beatrice, the Governor of the Isle of Wight, and the youngest daughter of Queen Victoria, opened Carisbrooke Castle Museum in the castle's newly restored gatehouse as a memorial to her late husband, Prince Henry of Battenberg. Over a hundred years later, the museum and its collection has grown and developed, and the charity Beatrice established continues to care for and share stories and artefacts from the Island's past with the public.

Princess Beatrice and Prince Henry of Battenberg

When Beatrice attended the wedding of her niece, Victoria in 1884, it was assumed that she herself would never marry. As the youngest daughter, it was considered her duty to remain with her mother. However, once she met Prince Henry of Battenberg, the brother of the groom and a member of a notably handsome family, there was an instant attraction. Beatrice's mother, the Queen, objected so vehemently to their love that she refused to speak to her daughter for months, and only communicated through written notes. She eventually agreed to the marriage on the one condition that the couple live with her, so that Beatrice could continue to be her mother's companion and secretary.

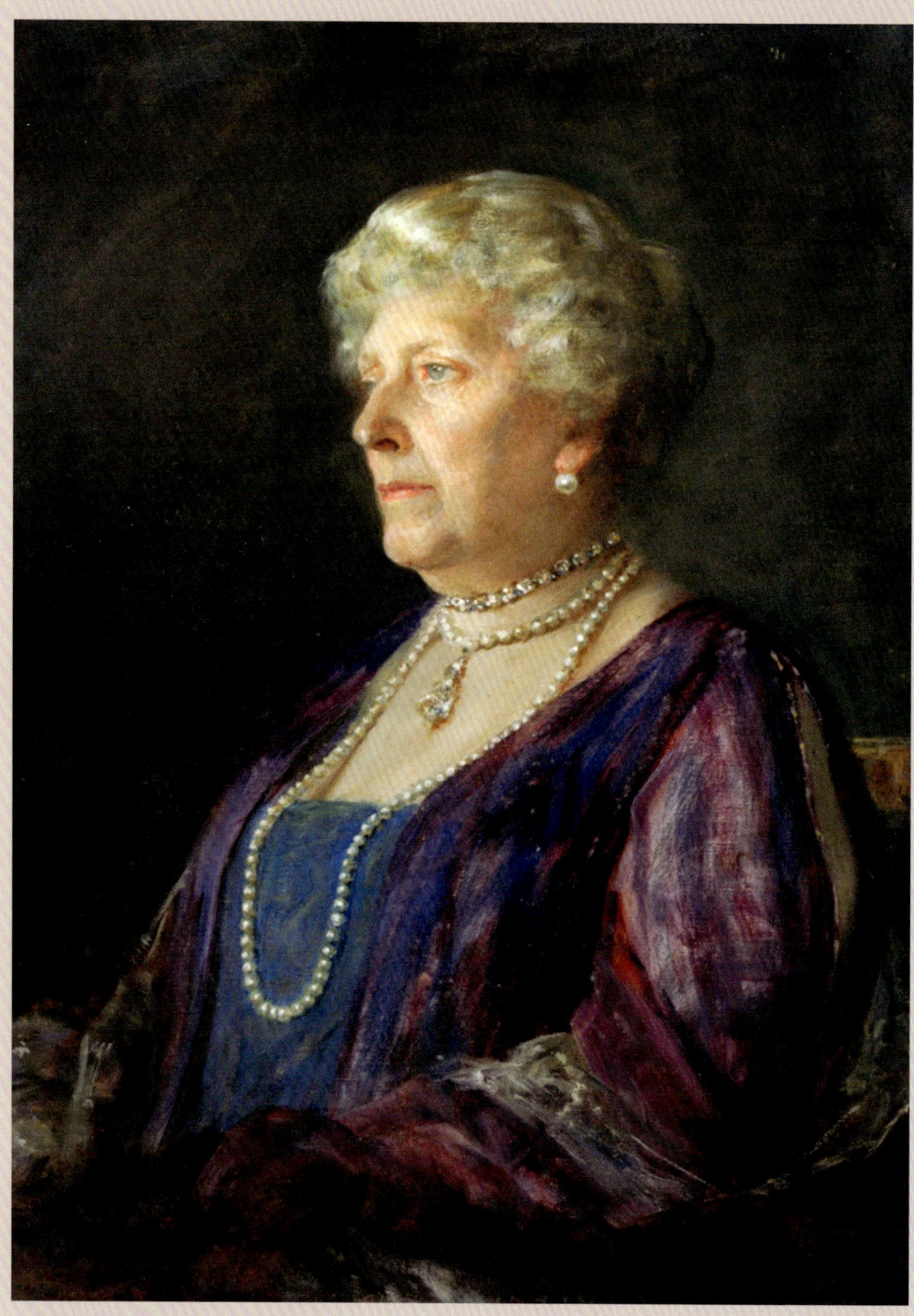

Princess Beatrice by Arthur Stockdale Cope, 1928
NETCC: P.1986.2124

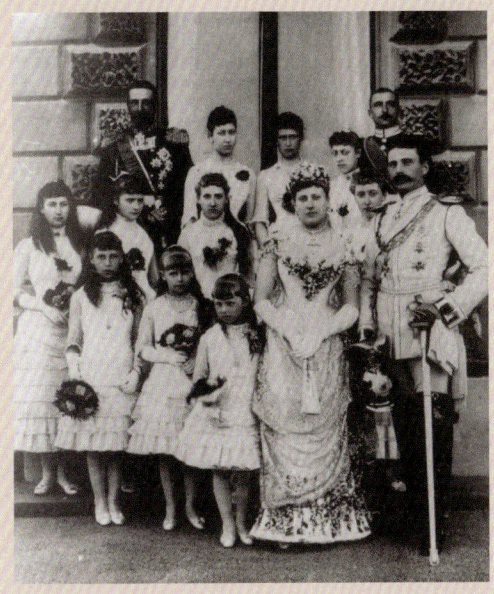

The wedding of Prince Henry and Princess Beatrice, 1885
NETCC: P.1986.2142

Beatrice and Henry were married on July 23rd, 1885, at St Mildred's Church in Whippingham. Henry was a morganic descendant of the Grand Ducal House of Hesse, meaning his parents were of unequal social status when they married – his father was a child of the reigning Grand Duke, Ludwig II of Hesse, while his mother Julia was a 'mere' countess. Upon their marriage, Queen Victoria made Henry a Knight of the Garter, conferring on him a status more equal to Beatrice's own. In 1885, he was also made the first Honorary Colonel of the Isle of Wight Rifles who were renamed 'Princess Beatrice's Volunteer Battalion' in the same year. The Queen and the newlyweds were often at Osborne House and the couple were both actively involved in Island life. Henry performed his duties with the Rifles with great enthusiasm and took part in several field days and marches, endearing himself to the men of the regiment. In 1889, he was made the Governor of Carisbrooke Castle and Captain-General and Governor of the Isle of Wight.

In 1895, Henry accompanied an expeditionary force to the Gold Coast of West Africa (modern-day Ghana). The men were to fight in the 4th Anglo-Ashanti War between British colonial powers who wanted to establish complete control of the area and its gold, and the Ashanti Empire who refused to surrender their sovereignty. Not long after the troops arrived malaria broke out in the camp and Henry fell ill. He was forced to return to England but never made it home, and he died on January 20th, 1896, on board the HMS Blonde. On the same day, the Ashanti leader King Prempeh surrendered and ended the war.

A Very Fitting Memorial

Beatrice had been married for a little more than 10 years when she found herself a young widow and mother, just as her mother Victoria had been. Attention quickly turned to how Henry might be appropriately memorialised. A committee was set up to consider a range of proposals including a new lifeboat, installing memorial windows in various Island churches, and establishing a Children's Wing at the County Hospital in Ryde. After several public meetings, the committee settled on the rebuilding of the chancel of Carisbrooke Parish Church (for which Charles Seely pledged £1000) and a memorial within the walls of the Castle. However, the plan to rebuild the chancel was abandoned because there were objections from the Society for the Protection of Ancient Buildings and several local people.

Princess Beatrice was asked to 'name the form which the memorial at Carisbrooke Castle should take', and although it is not known precisely how a final decision was reached, in a joint letter of July 20th, 1896, the secretary of the appeal committee and Mr Harbottle Estcourt, the Deputy Governor, wrote to the Office of Works:

"After much consideration it has been thought that a very fitting memorial, free from any objection, would be the restoration of the interior of the gate house of the Castle... At present the walls of the gate house are almost entire, but without roof or floors, open to the sky and exposed to the weather. The rooms when restored might be used for the preservation of manuscripts, drawings, plans, books of reference, and objects of interest connected with the Castle and antiquities of the Isle of Wight, and would be an attraction to the numerous visitors to the castle from all parts of the country and the colonies, and even from foreign countries."

Architect and antiquarian Percy Stone was commissioned to undertake the work, as Estcourt noted, he could be trusted to "treat the subject with a due regard to its antiquity." Percy had recently completed a study of Isle of Wight antiquities and was knowledgeable about historic buildings and churches across the Island. In 1904, under Beatrice's patronage, Percy also rebuilt the castle's chapel, St Nicolas-in-Castro as a memorial to Charles I, and then oversaw its re-dedication as the Isle of Wight County War Memorial after the First World War.

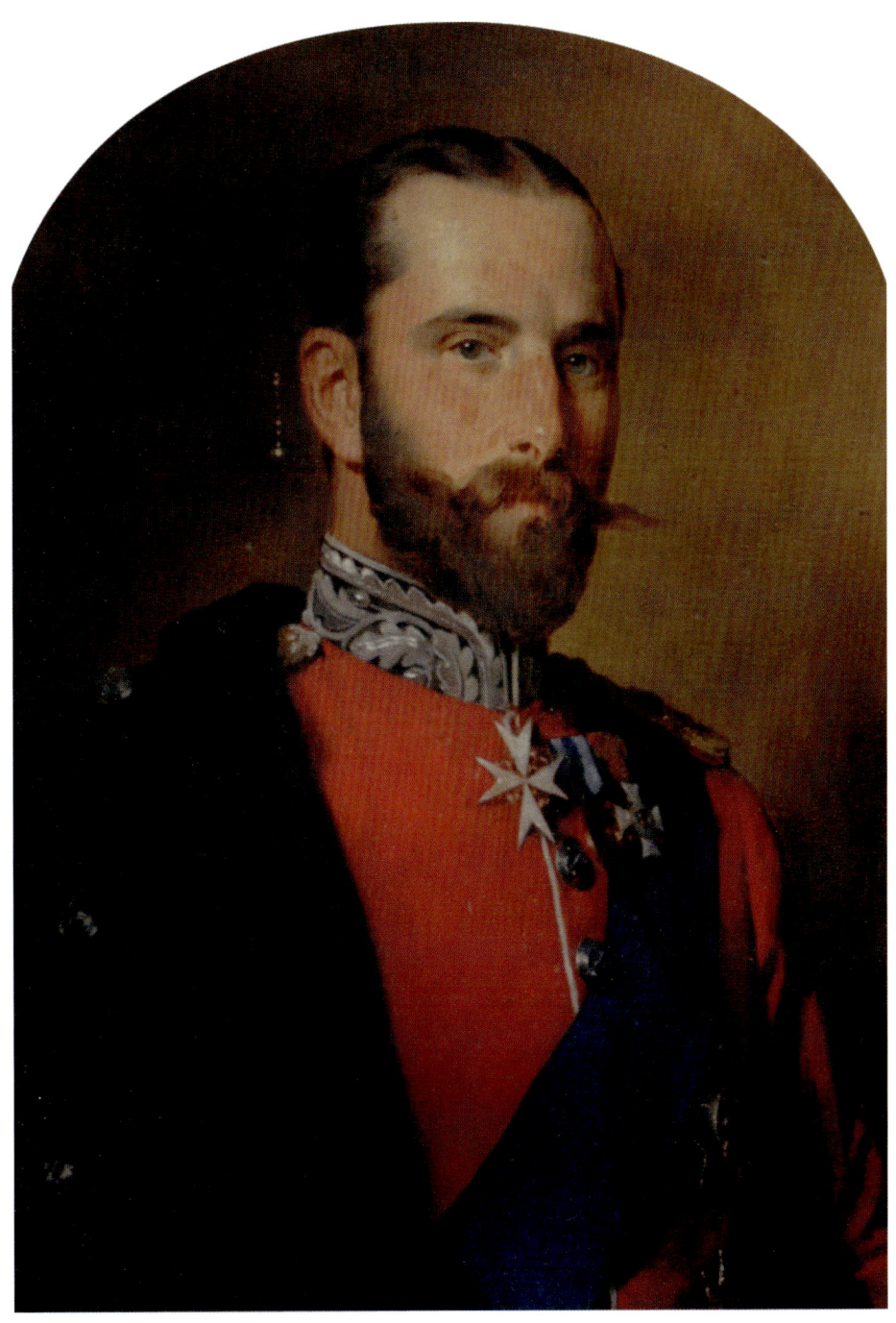

Prince Henry of Battenberg by Heinrich von Angeli, 1896
NETCC: P.1986.2125

The Castle had been suggested as a location for an Isle of Wight Museum ever since the founding of such an establishment was first debated. However, the idea was met with anger by some who felt it was unsuitable and too far from the County town. The museum had also been suggested as a memorial to Prince Albert, but it was only established after Henry's death. While the desire to memorialise Henry prompted its creation, the Museum and its collection have their roots in several earlier institutions and a longstanding local desire for an Isle of Wight history museum.

In 1820, the Isle of Wight Philosophical Society established the earliest recorded museum in Newport, which was a natural history collection held in rented rooms at the Isle of Wight Institution. However, by 1850 the collection needed a new home, and public meetings were held to discuss the possibility of a new public museum in Newport, which could be funded by donations and annual subscriptions. The new museum opened in 1853 at the Guildhall where there was more space allowing for the expansion of the collection. However, the organisation had to change location several times and financial difficulties led to its closure for over a decade until 1883 when the Newport Young Men's Literary Society acquired the collections and opened a new museum on Quay Street. By 1911, once again, financial problems forced a closure with most of the collection transferred to Carisbrooke Castle Museum.

The Museum's Early Years

Beatrice and the museum's early curators laid the foundations for the organisation that continues today. Two of the most influential individuals in Beatrice's lifetime were siblings Frank and Catherine Morey. In 1913, the same year Beatrice took up the Governor's House as her summer residence, Frank offered to take on the honorary curatorship (an unpaid position) with the help of his sister Catherine, who continued as Curator in her own right after Frank's death in 1925. From 1915 to 1927, they kept detailed day books which recorded their work and revealed the pleasures and challenges they encountered in looking after and developing the museum. Their concerns continue to echo in those of museum directors and curators a century later.

The museum had been established with no financial endowment, although this was not unusual and many local museums had to rely on the generous commitment of enthusiasts. Beatrice contributed money to special projects and the Moreys, the youngest children of the successful local timber merchant Henry Morey, made frequent journeys to London and helped to

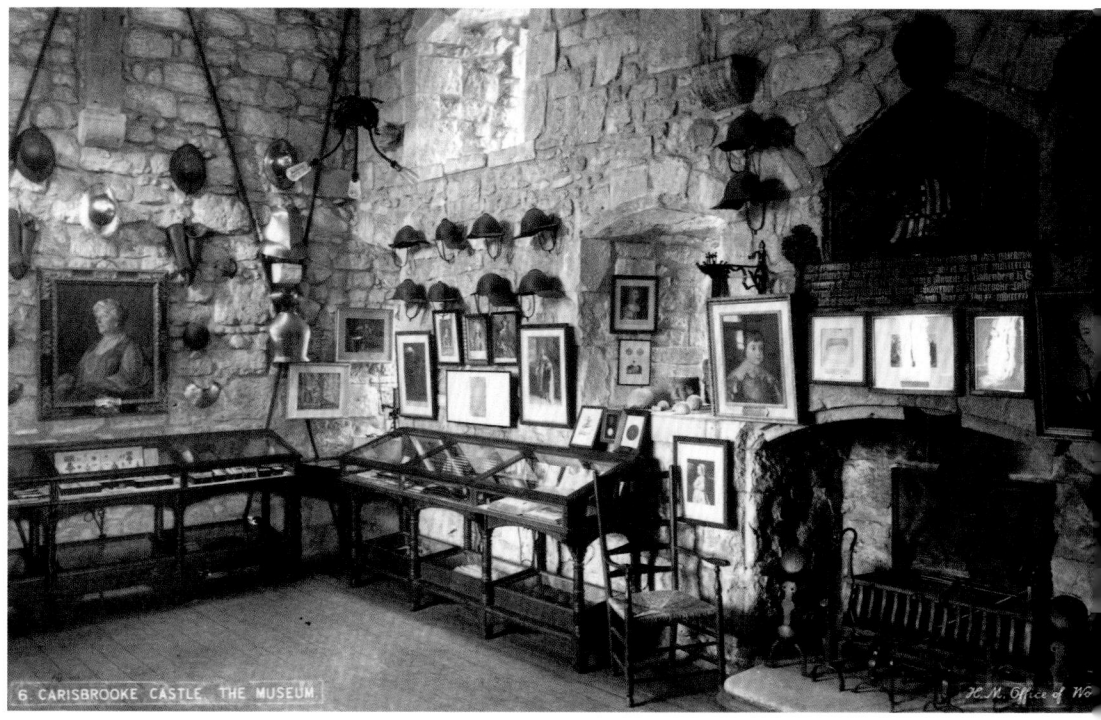

The Gatehouse Museum, about 1930
NETCC: 2003.5

fund excavations at their own expense. A permanent home within a castle in the care of the Office of Works was an undoubted benefit and an unusual one for a local history museum. However, the restored gatehouse was far from an ideal home for sensitive material and it was poorly maintained. The museum environment was a perpetual headache for the Moreys. Frank wrote in August 1915: "I asked the clerk of the works today if there was a prospect of the interior walls in the upper rooms being pointed and repaired to make them damp-proof. He replied that owing to the War such things must be postponed." Postponed they certainly were and things only got worse. In March 1919, 'the wall at the east end of the armoury was absolutely wet' and the stonework 'saturated'. Within a year, the roof was leaking too.

The defects in the building resulted in very high humidity which threatened the exhibits, and the day books frequently mention that dampness was affecting pictures, books and documents, which had to be taken home by Frank and Catherine to dry. The problem was made worse by the colonies of bats that inhabited the gatehouse and flitted around the walls of the rooms at night, leaving droppings on the armour and other exhibits.

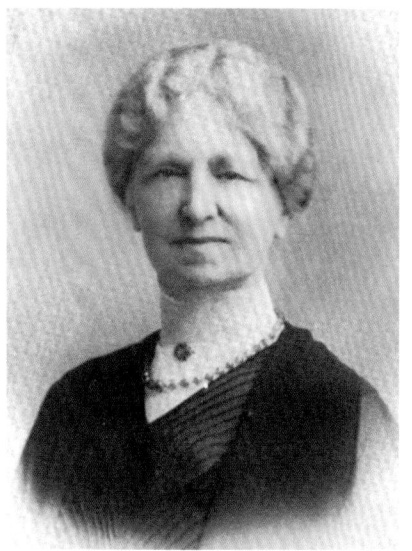
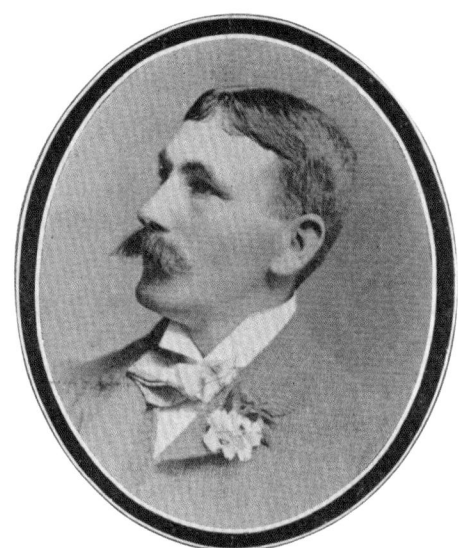

Catherine Morey

Percy Stone
NETCC: P.1986.2904.7

However, the Moreys were delighted to see the collections growing. Frank's first priority was to sort and clean artefacts from the Newport Museum. Having incorporated these into the collection, he next oversaw the transfer of objects from the old Ryde Museum, which was founded in 1857. He also acquired artefacts from excavations and bought objects through the funding provided by the Office of Works. The Moreys made regular visits to local scrap yards in hope of salvaging and preserving everyday objects illustrating Island life. Frank also had the foresight to collect some contemporary objects: when he encountered troops engaged in rifle practice on the downs, he kept some of their spent grenades for the museum. In his acquisitions, Morey applied a collecting policy, albeit a wide one, evidenced in a letter to a potential donor in which he wrote: "It looks interesting but has it anything to do with the Island?"

The Moreys also understood the importance of public access. They recorded visitor numbers regularly, and they were pleased to see these rising from 8,000 in 1914 to 25,000 after the end of the First World War. They often gave impromptu guided tours and noted the number of conversations they had with visitors, recording responses and comments about the displays.
After Frank's death, Princess Beatrice proposed that Catherine take over as curator and she did so until 1937 when ill health caused her to resign in favour

of her assistant, Hubert Poole. Unfortunately, his health also deteriorated, and Gerald Sherwin was curator from 1938 until his death in 1942. Rev. Harold Ewbank briefly succeeded Sherwin as curator until 1946, followed by the Rev. Edward Sydenham, who acted first as Rev. Ewbank's assistant and then as full honorary curator until 1948 alongside Rev. D. S. McKenzie until 1949. Without the details provided by the day books, it is less clear how the museum was run over these years. Beatrice stopped using the castle as her summer residence after 1938 but continued to be concerned for the museum she had founded. Just before her death in 1944, she set up a trust to take over its ownership and management with the intention of safeguarding the Museum's future.

A new home for the Museum

Conditions in the gatehouse had caused problems from the outset. Damp remained a particular issue and the building was becoming increasingly cramped. By 1948, the Trustees appointed by Princess Beatrice had decided that alternative accommodation was needed. They suggested to the Ministry of Works that the Governor's House, Beatrice's former residence, that at that time was temporarily being used as a youth hostel, should become the Museum's new home. Detailed proposals were prepared and sent to both the Ministry and Buckingham Palace. The decision rested with the King, George VI, and in 1949 the Trustees received notification that he had agreed to their request.

The museum's first full-time professional curator, Dudley Waterman was appointed and in 1950 alterations to the Governor's House began in readiness for the installation of new displays. Waterman proposed that the lower gallery should provide visitors with a chronologically arranged exhibition from the Island's geological past to the Jutes, which was an arrangement that lasted until the mid-1970s. The first room upstairs would largely be military themed and the second room would display social history objects ('byegones', as Mr Waterman termed them). Charles I 'relics' and the chamber organ would be housed in Princess Elizabeth's room, while another small room was designated the 'Print Room' for the display of prints and watercolours.

A year later, after protracted negotiations over showcases, heating, lighting and the appointment of custodians, the transfer of the Museum to the Governor's House was finally completed and the new museum officially opened on April 2nd, 1951 by the Island's Governor, the Duke of Wellington. The Times newspaper reported that 'in its new home this museum should play a useful part in the intellectual and cultural life of the Isle of Wight'.

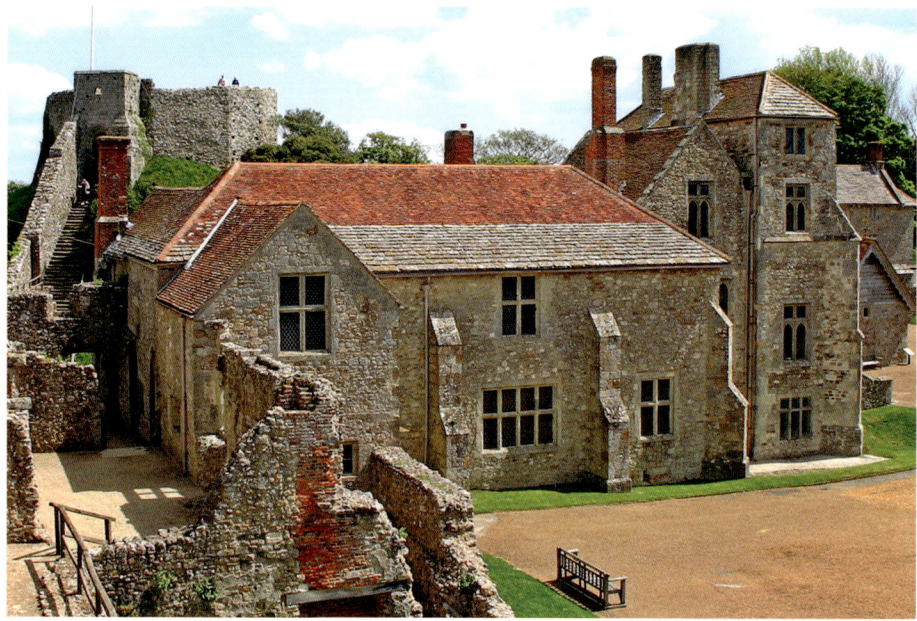

The Governor's House, Carisbrooke Castle

Collecting Isle of Wight History

When Princess Beatrice established the Museum, it was intended to be 'a treasury of objects illustrative of the history of the island', and in the 125 years since, the museum's collection has constantly grown and developed. Since the move to the Governor's House, the museum has been cared for by a further seven curators who have each bought their own interests and priorities to the collections, which now comprise over 35,000 objects ranging from the everyday to the exotic, and from utilitarian to pure novelty.

Historic objects survive and can enter museum collections in various ways, sometimes by accident, and other times by design. From its earliest days, most of the Museum's collection has been amassed through donations. Queen Victoria was an important early donor and gave significant items, including relics of Charles I. At the opening of the restored gatehouse Hallam, Lord Tennyson appealed to the Island's ancient families to deposit records and 'objects of antique workmanship' saying: "Here they will be safe; here they will be protected from damage or fire, and here they will be open to the inspection of the intelligent, the studious and the learned antiquary." Beatrice set an example by giving various items over the following years including a volume of Isle of Wight Rifles records, a gargoyle, and a plaster maquette of Marochetti's monument to Princess Elizabeth.

Because the Museum has rarely had the funds to make significant purchases, the collection has been largely shaped by what people have been willing to donate. In modern times, significant objects have entered the collection through the 'In Lieu of Inheritance Tax' scheme. More humble objects have also been given by local people, ranging from old keys to cooking pots. On occasion, objects were accepted despite the uncertainty of their connection to the Island, perhaps because of the status of the donor or other influential factors. Queen Mary purchased and gave a collection of Roman glass bottles she was told had been found on the Island. Frank Morey accepted them but after some research, placed them on display with a label acknowledging the uncertainty of them having been found locally.

Many of the objects which have found their way into the collection have been rare and lucky survivors. While some have been treasured and passed down through families for many generations, others owe their continued existence to other factors. From a carved ivory needlework stiletto lost between floorboards, to a piece of medieval music manuscript used to cover a book from a later period and a late nineteenth-century dress, that was adapted and repurposed by an amateur theatrical group. The demolition of old buildings has also provided a source of historic artefacts including objects (lost or possibly hidden) that were found during the demolition, as well as parts of the building itself. The demolition of the old St Thomas's church in Newport to make way for a new church in the 1850s caused the loss of a medieval building from the town, but it continues to exist through the fragments which were originally collected by the old Newport Museum.

The range of objects within the collection suggests how attitudes to what should be acquired has changed over time and under the influence of different curators. Today, the museum has a clear collecting policy that focuses exclusively on acquiring items that help tell the specific history of the Island, but in years past many objects were collected for their general historic interest. At one point in the 1960s, the Curator and Chairman decided to purchase a collection of old woodwind instruments from a vendor in Portsmouth. Despite the reservations of the Trustees due to the "point of principle" that the policy of the museum had been to "confine their exhibits to objects which had a definite connection with the Isle of Wight", the purchase was ultimately confirmed and it was agreed that the museum would seek to establish a collection of early musical instruments, although this is not a policy that appears to have been pursued with any particular commitment or enthusiasm.

For a local history museum to remain relevant in the 21st century it needs to be able to tell the stories of local people and their lives. Collecting contemporary artefacts is important in achieving this goal and is a task that the museum actively pursues. This might include collecting items that build on the strength of the existing collection, such as the acquisition of locally made contemporary ceramics to complement the existing holdings of 20th-century local ceramics. As well as trying to ensure significant local events are marked by the addition of items to the collection, such as objects associated with the Covid-19 pandemic or the first Isle of Wight Pride event.

One Hundred Treasures and Curiosities

The result of the Museum's long history is a sometimes-eclectic mix of historic objects which is reflected in the wide variety of objects selected in this book. The idea for the publication came in the lead-up to the museum's 125th anniversary in 2023 and was envisioned as a fitting way of celebrating not only the Museum's history but also that of the Island. The objects included have been selected to enable us to share not only some of the Isle of Wight's most historic and significant stories but also some of the unusual and quirky tales from the island's past.

In preparing the selection, in which only one hundred objects from the many thousands in the collection could feature, we considered a variety of factors and approaches. The diverse, but not necessarily representative, nature of the collections makes any kind of comprehensive chronology of local history difficult. We were conscious that we wanted to celebrate all the key areas of the collection and to ensure the selection from these different aspects was balanced with none taking undue precedence. We also decided early on that, with a few exceptions, we would primarily focus on objects rather than the museum's fascinating and extensive collections of photographs and documents, the former of which could easily fill several publications on their own. We wanted the book to be a visual feast, so how well an object could be reproduced in a photograph was an important consideration. We thought about the stories different objects could tell but have also included interesting objects of uncertain provenance. Long lists were edited and then whittled further until a final selection was eventually reached. Some beautiful objects without a clear story to tell fell by the wayside whilst new research discoveries secured the place of objects we had previously known little about. And just as the collection has been shaped over the years by the people caring for it, the personal interests of the authors, our tastes, priorities, and affection for certain objects, have inevitably helped determine the final list.

The selection opens with a ceremonial key designed by Percy Stone for the museum's first home in the castle gatehouse. While it then features some of the oldest traces of the Island's earliest inhabitants (Palaeolithic stone hand axes) and closes with one of the most recently made and acquired (a set of homemade scrubs made during the Covid-19 pandemic), the objects have not been organised in a strict chronology. We have attempted to find themes and connections between groups of objects which tell a particular story (for example that of Charles I and his daughter or the Island's rich maritime past) or have paired objects together where their connection or juxtaposition generates a particular resonance. As you explore the following pages, we hope you enjoy discovering the Island's history through these treasures and curiosities.

100 Treasures & Curiosities

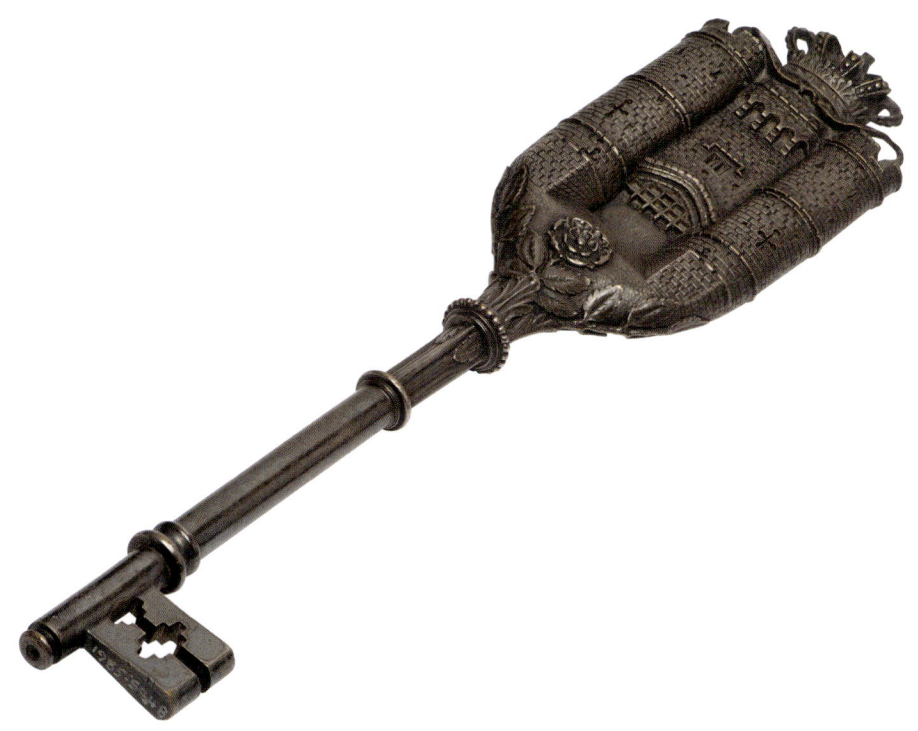

Ceremonial key

NETCC: 1985.5248

Given by Earl Mountbatten of Burma, 1969

This silver-plated key was designed by architect Percy Stone to commemorate the opening of the newly restored castle gatehouse in 1898. This gatehouse was the first home of Carisbrooke Castle Museum, which was founded as a memorial to Princess Beatrice's late husband, Prince Henry who was known to the family as Liko.

In her journal, Queen Victoria noted Beatrice "had been to Carisbrooke Castle early in the afternoon to be present at the opening of the museum, which has been restored and adapted as such, as an Island memorial to dear Liko. [The museum] is to contain relics and Island antiquities. The ceremony was I hear very touching and over 2000 people were there. It was very trying for poor dear Beatrice, though she was so touched at all the kindness shown."

Sponsored by John and Hazell Sutton - Elmstone Engineering Ltd

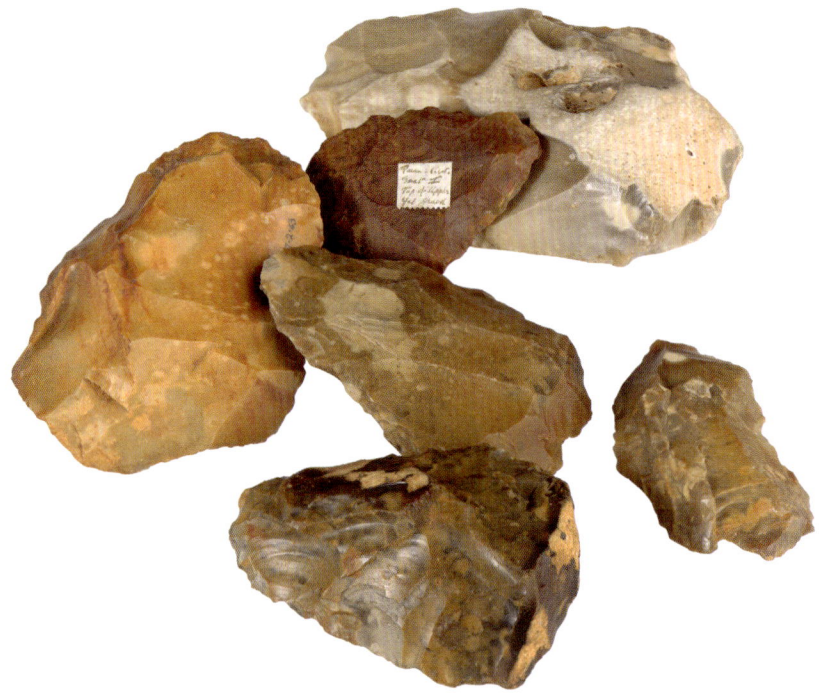

Palaeolithic hand axes

IWCMS : 877.2.41; 877.2.43; 877.5.1; 877.5.3; 877.5.11; 877.5.25

Hand axes dating from the Palaeolithic era provide the very earliest evidence of humans on the land that would form the Isle of Wight. These were made by Neanderthal people 400,000–30,000 years ago, and they would have been used for chopping or smashing meat, plants, wood and other materials. The people who used them were nomadic, following migrating wild animals and the plants that grew in the changing, warming environment. Rising sea levels eventually flooded the English Channel and Solent River, separating the Island from the mainland and creating the first true Islanders, hunter-gatherers who gradually became a settled farming community. In 1912, Hubert Poole (later a curator of the museum) helped workmen digging a new gravel pit at Great Pan Farm to identify these early stone tools.

Sponsored by Paul & Jo Bingham

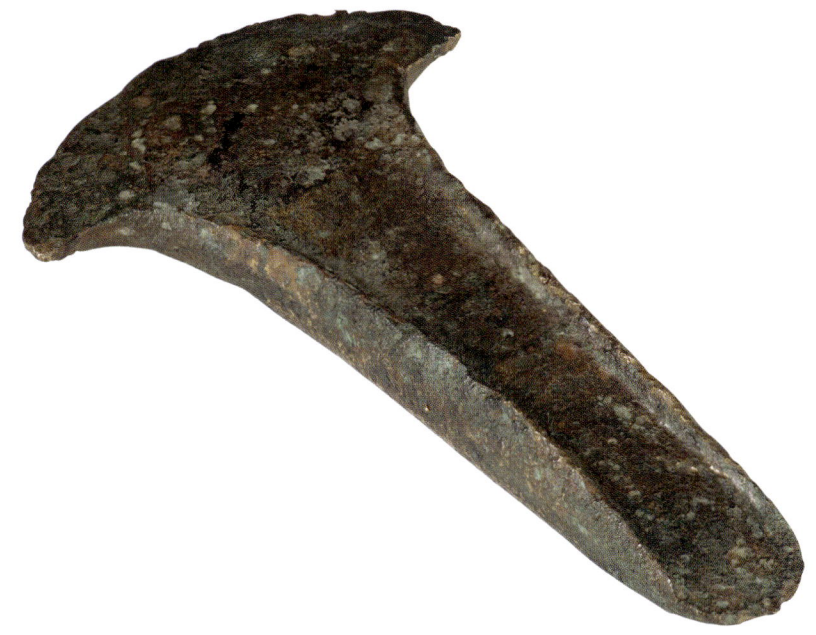

Bronze Age flanged axe

IWCMS : 51..1

This axe head is made of copper alloy and would originally have been fitted with a wooden handle, that was glued, and bound together. The Bronze Age saw the introduction of metalworking and metal tools with the Island ideally placed to facilitate the trade of metals by sea. It was found in 1942 as part of a hoard of axe heads, spear heads, and dagger blades at Moons Hill, Freshwater. It was discovered after a local farmer's cattle trod down an earthen bank by a stream, revealing one of the axe heads. Hoards of valuable objects were often intentionally buried for safekeeping but then, for some reason, not retrieved. Studies have suggested that this hoard may have been a ritual deposit, left as a gift to the gods.

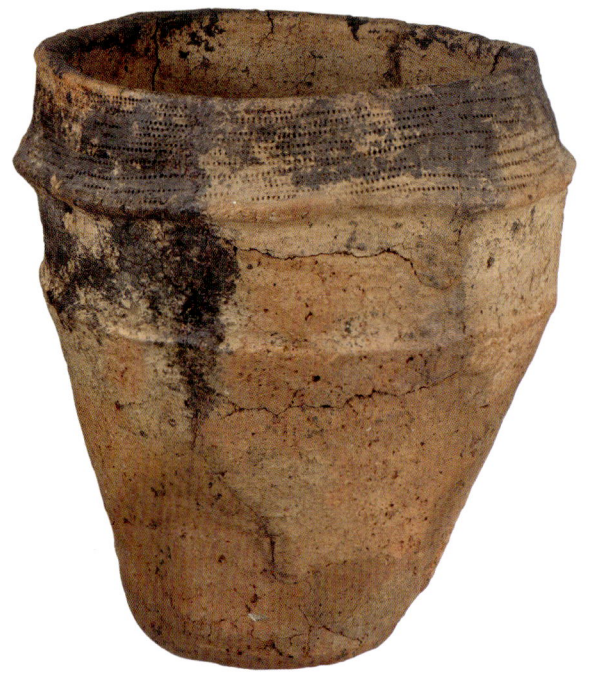

Bronze Age collared urn

IWCMS : 664.1.4

This hand-made fired-clay vessel was discovered at Week Down near Ventnor, and dates to the Bronze Age, between 4,300 and 2,700 years ago. It is a cremation (or cinerary) urn and contained the ashes of a dead person buried in a burial mound (or barrow). This style of vessel is common throughout Britain, and has a distinctive heavy overhanging rim or collar that is usually decorated – for example, imprinted with a pointed implement, the potter's fingernail or a piece of cord.

Burial mounds are recorded as having been opened in the search for treasure as far back as 1237. Nineteenth-century antiquarians were also active in their investigation of these structures and they have now nearly all been disturbed and their grave goods removed. This example was excavated in 1968.

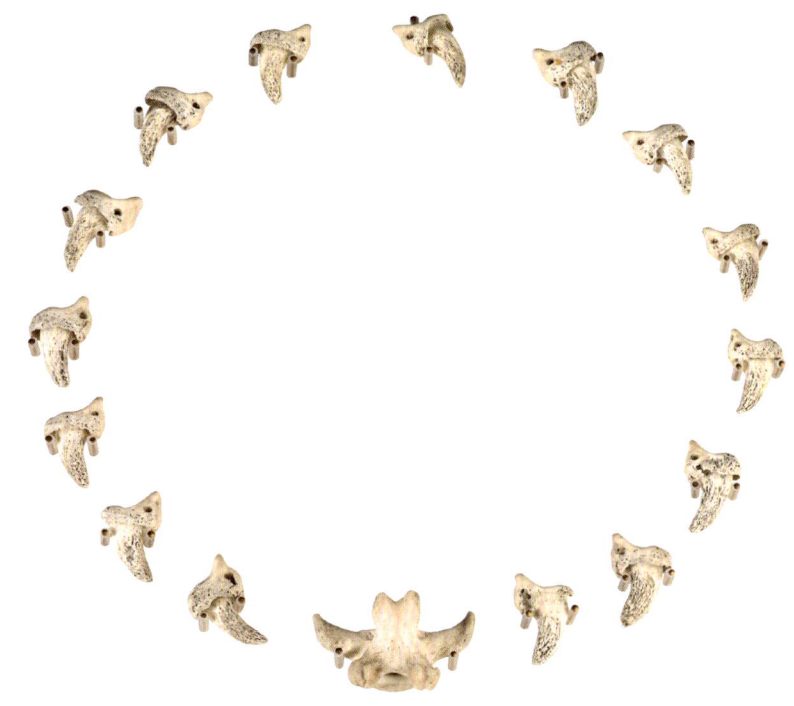

Wolf claw necklace

IWCMS : 485..35

This necklace is one of the most mysterious artefacts in the museum's collection. It is made from wolf claws and a single vertebra (backbone) of a small animal, possibly also a wolf. It is a rare survivor and unusually well preserved, perhaps because of the alkaline environment of the chalky ground around Mount Joy where it was unearthed. The claws may have come from one single animal or a number, with claws of similar sizes selected to hang together. The necklace would have been a powerful symbol, perhaps worn as a protective charm or a hunting trophy.

Frank Morey recorded that there was evidence of a Bronze Age round barrow at the site near Carisbrooke, which had been covered by a cemetery. During the digging of graves, Bronze Age and Iron Age items were unearthed, but while Morey records that this necklace came from a barrow and entered the collection in 1918, we don't know exactly how or where it was found.

Sponsored for Ability Dogs 4 Young People IoW

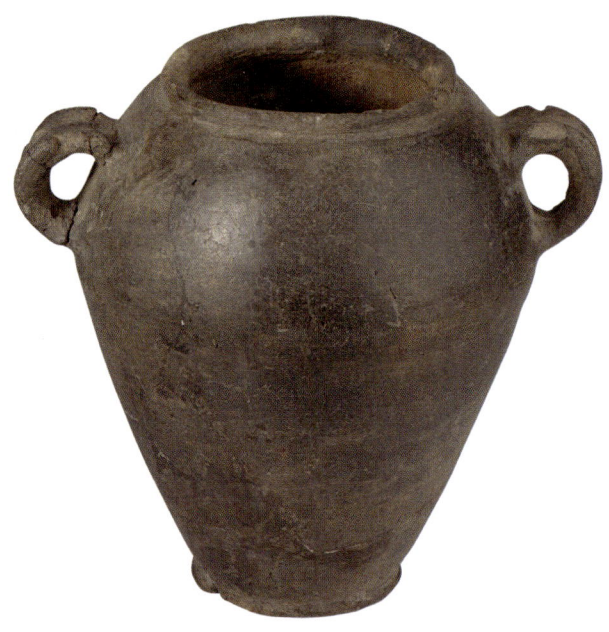

Roman Vectis Ware pot

IWCMS : 49.0.1
Given by Robert Walker, 1898

In 1898, workers digging sand discovered this twin-handled fired-clay pot in the stone-lined grave of a Romano British woman at Sheepwash Farm, Freshwater. Known as a cist, these types of graves often contained the body with items alongside that indicated the person's status in life, such as this pot, which may have stored food. Vectis Ware is a hard, hand-made pottery, which is most commonly very dark grey in colour due to burnishing - a pottery treatment in which the surface of the pot is polished using a hard smooth surface. Under Roman rule, the Island was a prosperous agricultural centre, with evidence of eight Romano-British villas (farmsteads).

An explosion of interest in archaeology during the Victorian period led to the discovery of many sites and artefacts on the Island. Princess Beatrice was fascinated by archaeology and visited local dig sites including the one at Sheepwash Farm. She asked that finds be donated to the museum and sent a royal carriage to transport them.

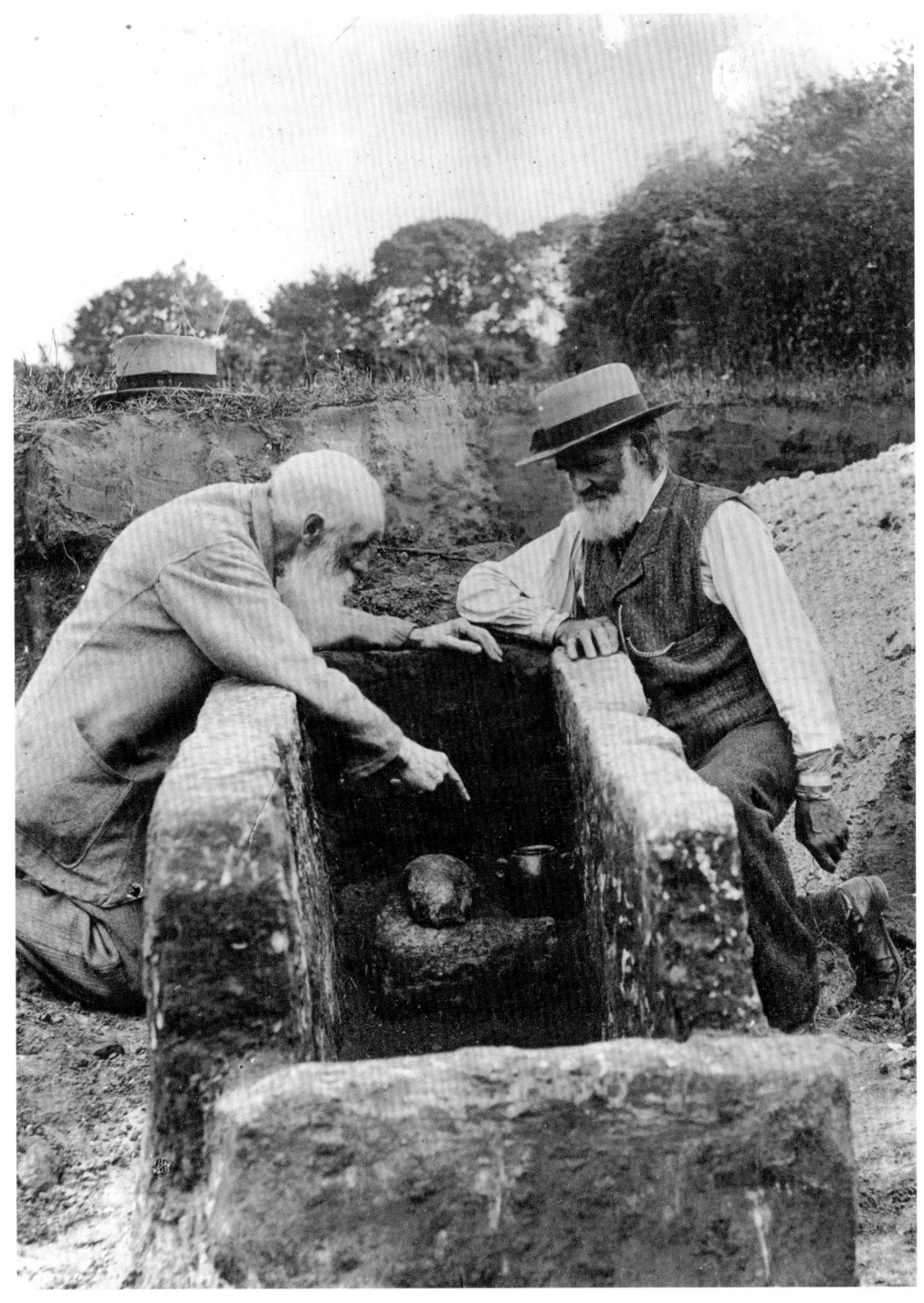

Antiquarian Robert Walker at the Romano British burial at Sheepwash Farm, 1898
NETCC: P.1986.797

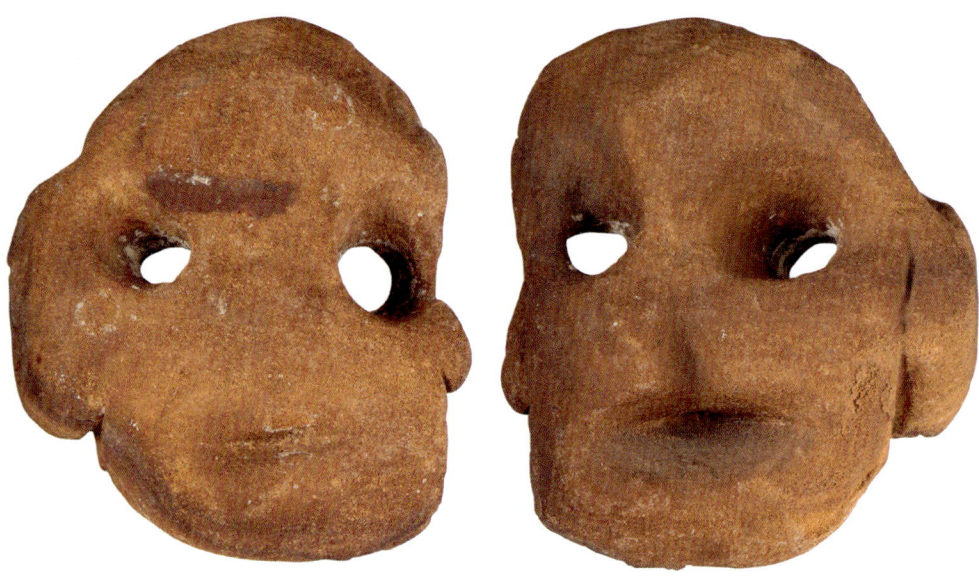

Stone Janus head

IWCMS : 1173.999.1

Janus is the Roman god of gates and doors, beginnings and endings, and is represented by two faces each looking in opposite directions. He was worshipped at beginnings such as births, marriages, sowing crops, and the start of the harvest. Two eyeholes have been bored all the way through this piece of iron sandstone and other features are roughly carved into its opposite faces. Another carved stone head was found at Luccombe and would probably have been displayed within a wall niche perhaps in a shrine or sanctuary, but the small size of this item would have made it more portable. It was found at Culver Cliff during military operations in 1952.

Sponsored for Carolyn Stirling

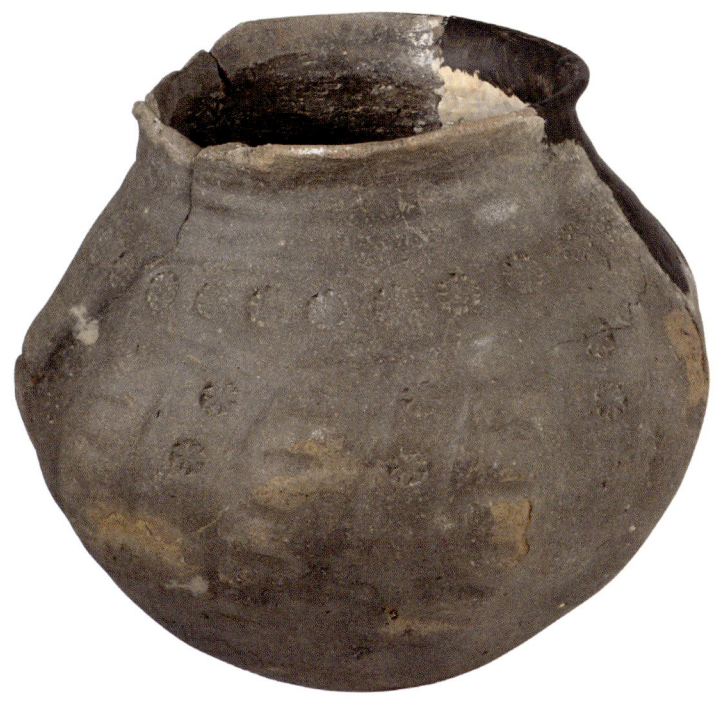

Anglo-Saxon urn

IWCMS : 124..3

During the Anglo-Saxon period, pottery vessels such as this were made using simple thumb-pinching and coil-building techniques, methods which had not changed much since the Iron Age. They could be plain or decorated, depending on their use and the status of their owner. Decoration could be applied with incised lines or stamped with geometric patterns like this one from Shalcombe Down.

The Anglo-Saxon cemetery at Shalcombe was located on the slope of a chalk ridge and faced another significant cemetery at Chessell. There were a variety of burial types on the site including inhumation (burial of a body) and burial of cremated remains in cists (stone-lined graves). Although its discovery was not documented, it is most likely that this vessel was a cremation urn, which was placed inside a barrow that contained an older Bronze Age burial.

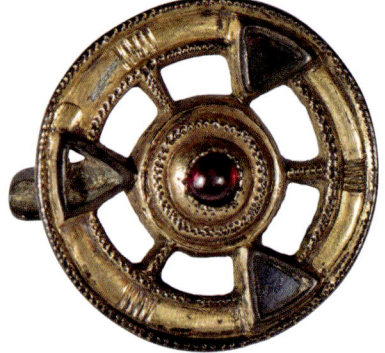 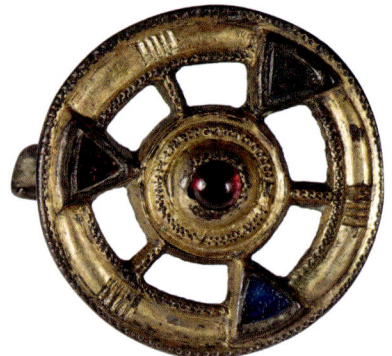

Anglo-Saxon keystone brooches

IWCMS : 128..1

In 1816 John Dennett recovered this pair of Anglo-Saxon gilded-silver disc brooches mounted with garnet and glass from a chalk pit where they had fallen when a barrow at Shalcombe collapsed in about 1745. The garnets in these brooches probably came from India or Sri Lanka via Mediterranean traders. At a time when travel over water could be quicker than over land, the Island was ideally placed at the centre of routes allowing an exchange of ideas and a trade in goods. Links with the continent can be seen in the design and craftsmanship of personal ornaments and decorations such as brooches. Styles from the Frankish empire (modern France) and materials from further afield were used to create beautiful and expensive ornaments.

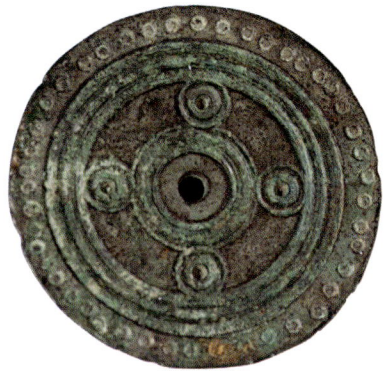 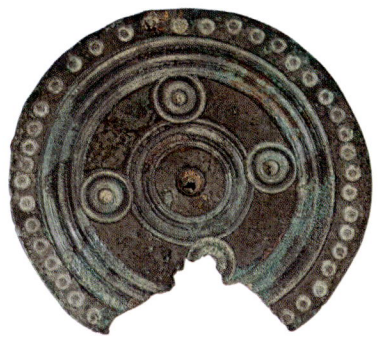

Anglo-Saxon bronze disc brooches

IWCMS : 124..1

Circular disc brooches were popular in early Anglo-Saxon England. Worn in pairs on the chest and used to fasten clothing, they could be simply decorated with a geometric pattern or more ornamented with inlaid stones or glass. These examples with their punched and incised decoration date to the fifth or sixth century and were excavated from a burial mound (or barrow) on Shalcombe Down by Sir Leonard Holmes and John Dennett in 1816.

After the withdrawal of the Romans, groups of Germanic people from continental northern Europe such as the Angles, Jutes and Saxons (collectively known as Anglo-Saxons) crossed the North Sea and settled in parts of southern and eastern Britain. Far from being a 'dark age' between the end of Roman rule and the Norman Conquest, artefacts from this period tell a story of a sophisticated society with skilled craftspeople and international connections to Europe and beyond.

Sponsored by Leslie J Farrow

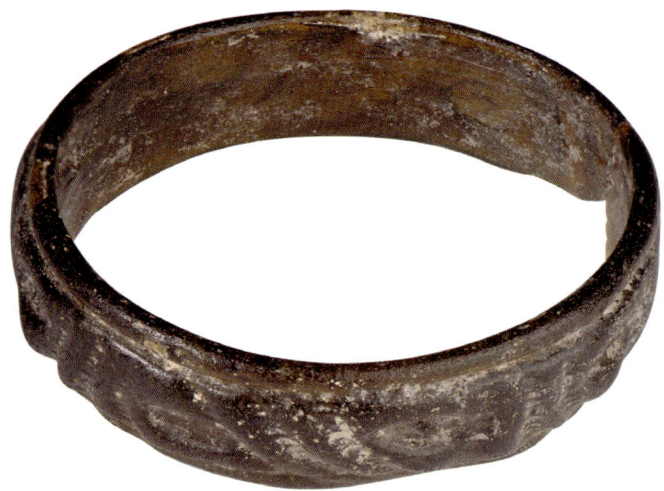

Anglo-Saxon glass armlet

IWCMS : 138..3
Transferred from Winchester City Museum, 1953

The Anglo-Saxons used a range of both functional and decorative glass objects such as beads and jewellery. This olive-green glass armlet was discovered on the arm of a female skeleton in an Anglo-Saxon burial on Chessell Down. It dates to the fifth or sixth century and is one of only a handful of other armlets of this period known in England. This example, which has moulded decorations of chevrons and rings, is the most ornate.

During the nineteenth century, the increasing interest of local antiquarians in archaeology led to the discovery of many stunning Anglo-Saxon artefacts. Most were found in cemeteries and provide some of the best clues to understanding the everyday lives of these ancient people. One of the most significant sites was a cemetery on Chessell Down. Originally unearthed by diggers collecting marl (a type of clay soil used as a fertiliser), it contained over 130 burials and produced a wide variety of grave goods.

Sponsored by Margaret Moore

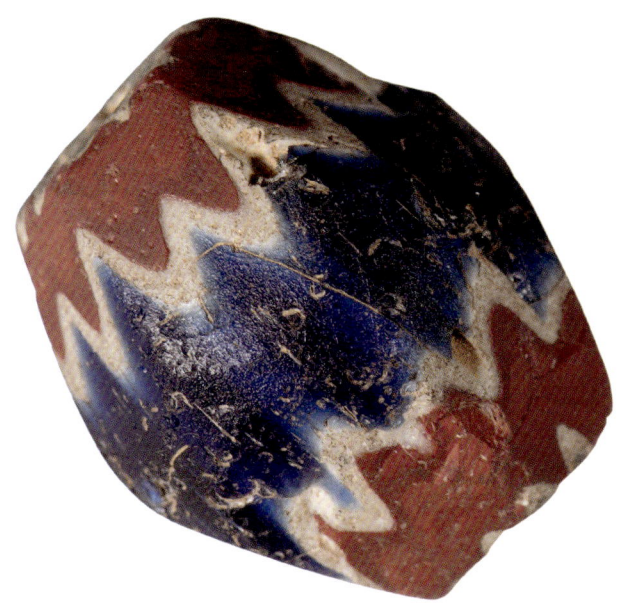

Chevron glass bead

IWCMS : 1397..1
Given by Mrs Mitchell, 1918

This biconical glass bead was discovered near St George's Church in Arreton. People have been worshipping on this site since at least the eleventh century, but the current church may be a successor to an earlier late-Saxon church. Beads of this style are found throughout the world and this example may date from any time from the Early Medieval to Post-Medieval periods (800-1500CE). Without a record of the context in which it was found its precise date cannot be determined. When it entered the museum collection in 1918, the Curator Frank Morey noted: "It is interesting owing to the uncertainty as to its origin & date for it is a curious thing that similar beads to this specimen have occurred in various parts [of the world] ... The whole thing is most puzzling, but I suppose the mystery will be cleared up some day."

Walrus ivory tableman

NETCC: 1985.2963
Purchased, 1960

This is a very finely carved counter, or tableman, for a game of tables dating from around 1130-40. It was found down a well on the Isle of Wight in 1732. The carving shows a Norman knight wearing a mail coat and conical helmet. He is standing on a drawbridge outside a Norman castle topped with battlements. This is likely just one of a full set of counters and its fine carving suggests it belonged to someone with wealth who could not only afford such an item, but also could engage in leisurely activities. Games were seen as a chivalrous pursuit for the nobility and a way of developing strategic thinking.

Tables was a game of mixed luck and skill in which two players competed to get their fifteen men across the board first whilst blocking the moves of their opponent. The board was similar to a modern backgammon board and was known as a 'pair of tables'. Each 'table' had six points along its opposite edges. Players rolled the dice to determine the movement of pieces, moving men along the board according to the throws of the dice. Single pieces were vulnerable to capture, but multiple stacked pieces were secure and stopped an opponent from occupying the position.

Sponsored by Pauline Petrie

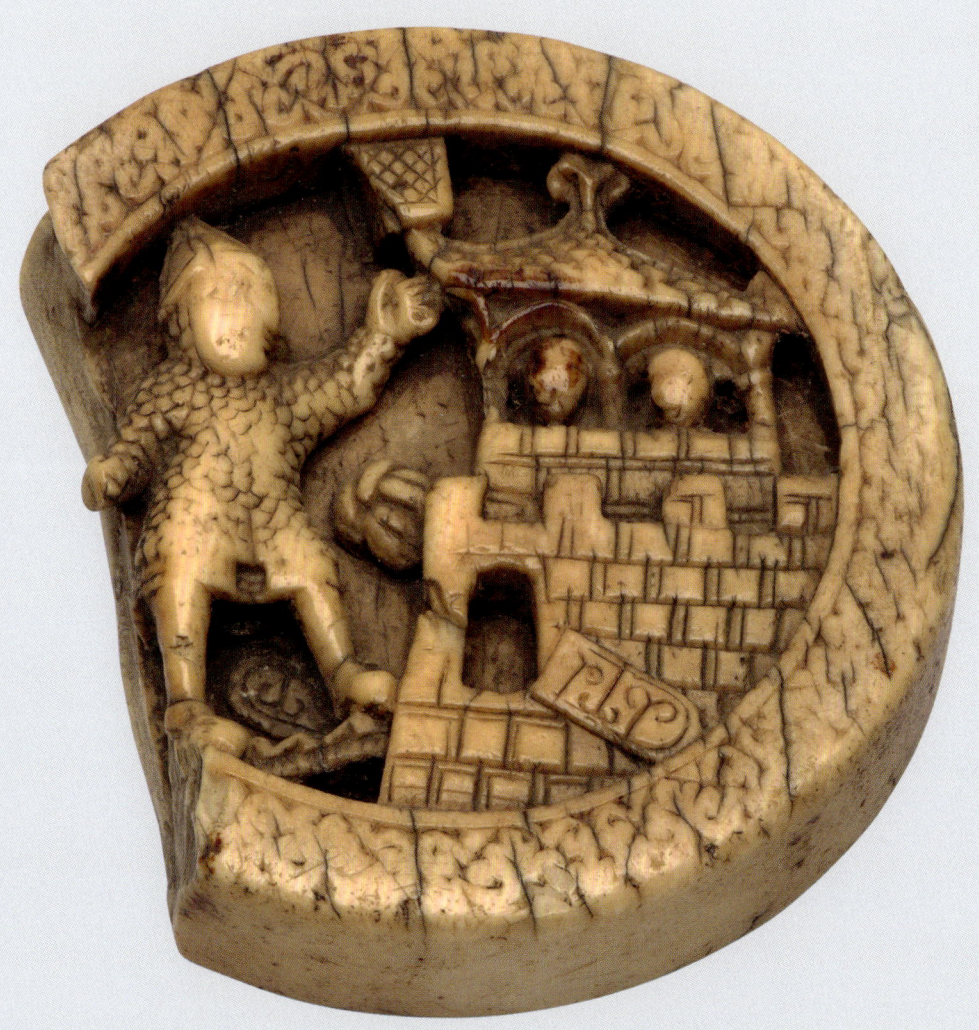

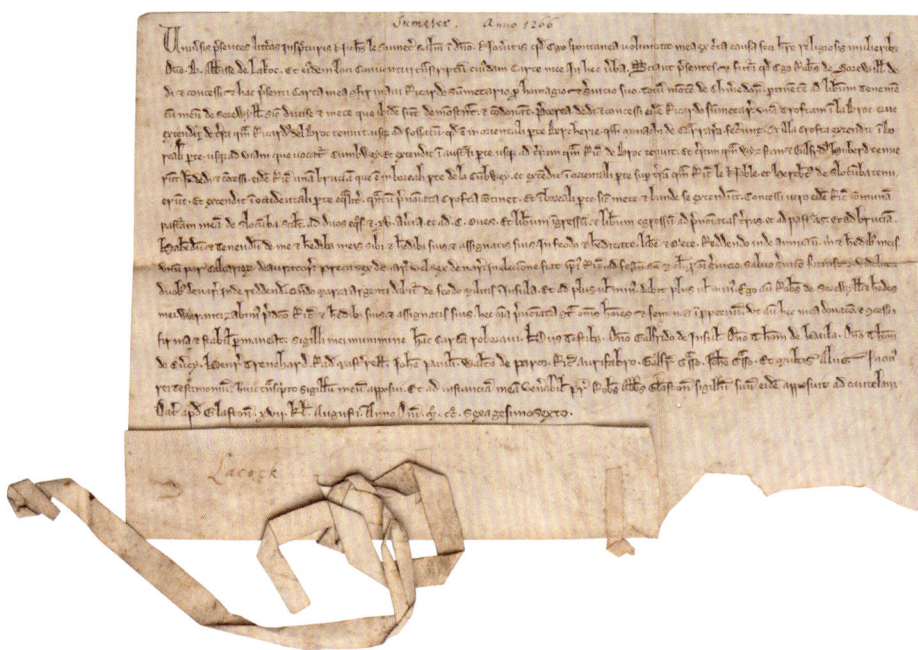

Charter of Nicholas le Sumpter

NETCC: D.1986.940

Dating from 1266, this medieval charter is the oldest document in the museum's collection. It appears to relate to the granting of grazing rights on land just outside Shorwell. In the thirteenth century, Amice, the Countess of Devon gave the manor of North Shorwell to Beatrice of Kent, the Abbess of Lacock Abbey. Amice, the mother of Isabella de Fortibus who held the lordship of the Isle of Wight from 1262 to 1293, perhaps made the gift as an act of religious devotion. Local landowners, including Nicholas le Sumpter who is named in this document, also gave land surrounding the manor. It is written in Latin with abbreviations often used in legal documents. Few charters from this period have survived, making this an important resource for historians of the medieval Island.

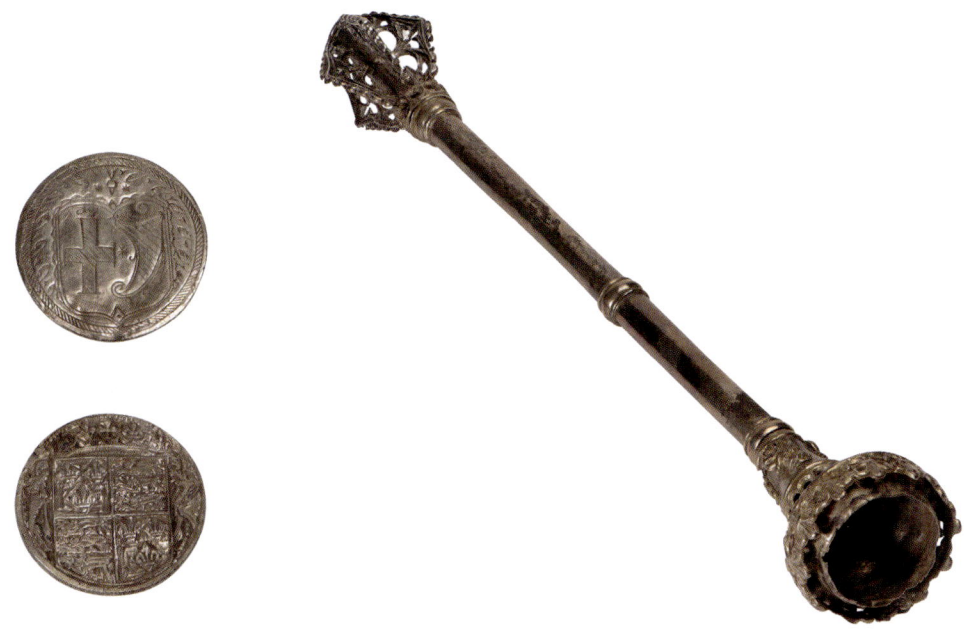

Newtown mace

NETCC: 1985.5189

Accepted by HM Government in lieu of Inheritance Tax and allocated to Carisbrooke Castle Museum, 2004, with additional funding from The Heritage Lottery Fund Resource/V&A Purchase Grant Fund, The Friends of Carisbrooke Castle Museum and The Simeon Family Trust.

Above - the engraved disc showing the Commonwealth 'State Arms' (top) and the arms of Henry VII (bottom).

This silver mace is more than 500 years old and dates from the reign of Henry VII, in the late 1400s. It comes from the ancient borough of Newtown and was used as a symbol of authority on civic occasions. Newtown, then known as Francheville, was founded in 1256 but much of the town was destroyed in 1377 by invading French forces. It never recovered its economic importance but civic life flourished. There is a fine eighteenth-century town hall, and the borough was represented by two members of Parliament until the Great Reform Act of 1832 swept away the so-called 'rotten boroughs'.

Perhaps the most interesting feature of the mace is a two-sided disc that is inserted at one end. During the English Civil War, the Lord of the nearby manor of Swainston, Sir Thomas Barrington, supported Parliament. He apparently removed the plate engraved with the Royal coat of arms and engraved the Commonwealth arms on the reverse, ensuring that whatever the outcome of the war might be, the mace could show Newtown's 'loyal' support.

Sponsored by Michael Paler

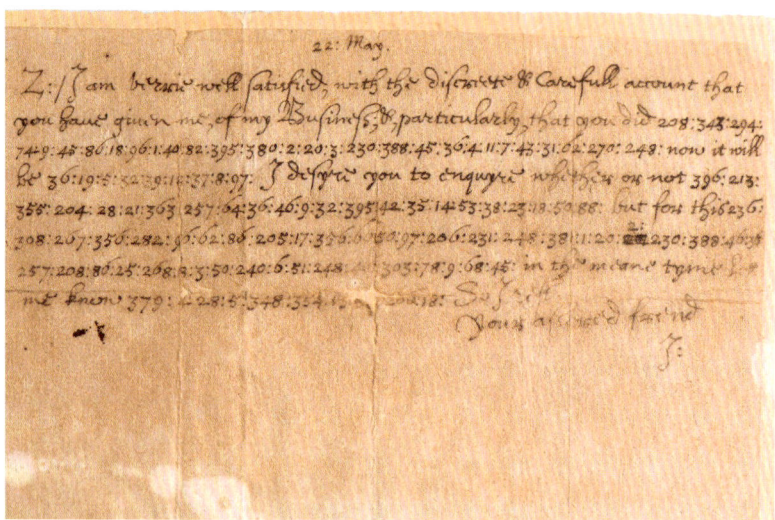

Letter written in code by Charles I

NETCC: D.1986.948

During his imprisonment at Carisbrooke, Charles relied on letters smuggled to and from the Castle to keep him informed of European politics, Parliament's plans and to plot his escape attempts. These letters were often written in code to frustrate his enemies, using a combination of plain English (written in disguised handwriting), a number code and a series of single letters representing the names of his allies.

This letter, written entirely in code apart from a few words in English, was addressed to Sir Edward Worsley, a Royalist accomplice whose code name was 'Z'. Its date, 22nd of May 1648, and the extensive use of code suggest it may include details of an escape plan, which was to happen on the 28th of May, but which ended up failing as two of the guards bribed by the Royalists revealed the plot. Charles' number code was relatively complex and some of his cyphers, including the one used in this letter, are still baffling code breakers to this day.

Sponsored by Jonathan Bacon

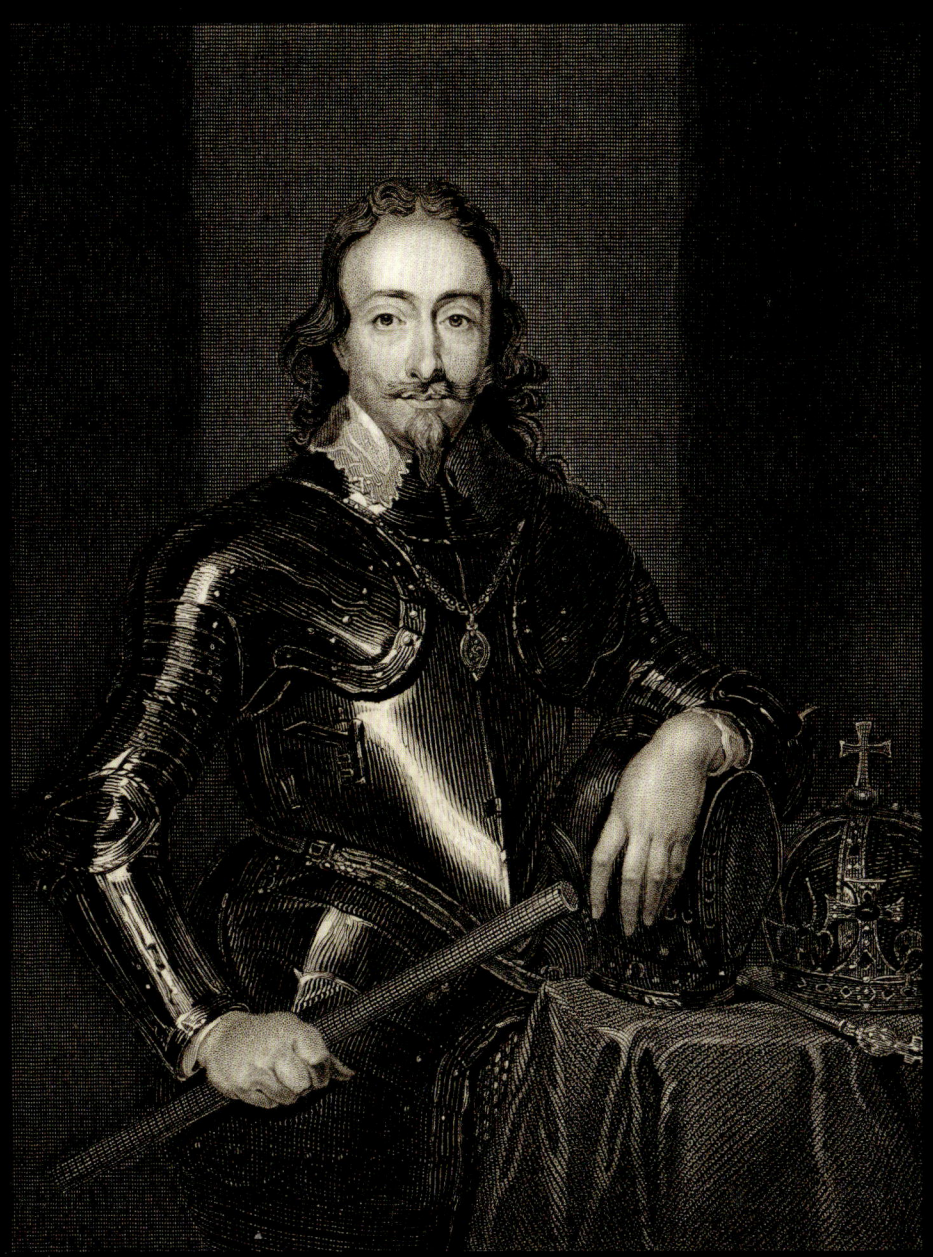

King Charles I, engraved by John Henry Robinson, after Sir Anthony van Dyck, 1828
NETCC: P.1986.1070

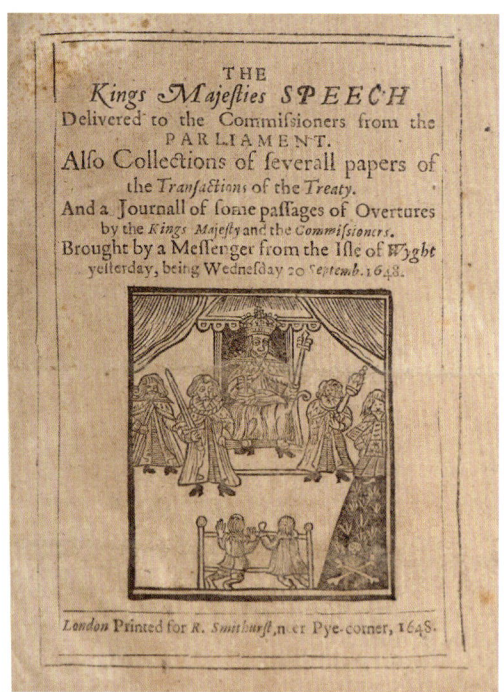

Civil War news sheet

NETCC: D.1986.5

During the English Civil War (1642–1651) royal censorship temporarily collapsed leading to an abundance of printed material. The war created a hunger for news and as more people were able to read than ever before, both Royalists and Parliamentarians published regular news sheets. For those who could not read, woodcut illustrations were included and were another effective form of propaganda.

This news sheet reports on the early negotiations at the Treaty of Newport in September 1648. On September 6th, King Charles was paroled and taken from Carisbrooke Castle to Newport to meet with representatives of Parliament. Negotiations lasted for several weeks but ultimately failed. At dawn on the 30th of November, the King was abruptly woken, put into a coach and taken by ferry to Hurst Castle. From there Charles travelled to London for his trial and eventual execution.

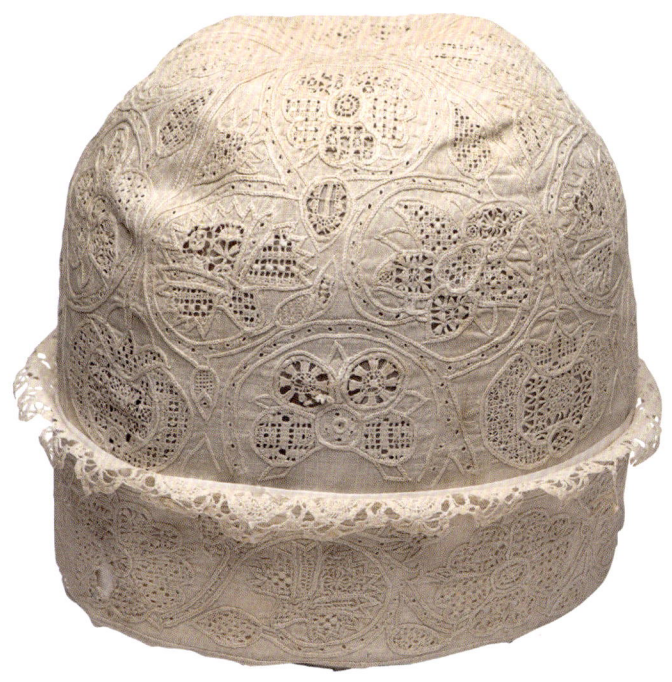

Charles I's linen nightcap

INETCC: 1985.3790

Given by Queen Victoria, 1899

This seventeenth-century nightcap is said to have been worn by Charles on the night before his execution and was given to the museum by Queen Victoria. Charles spent his last night at St James's Palace accompanied by his attendant Thomas Herbert who slept on a pallet beside the King's bed. The King rose before dawn and woke Herbert and told him he had 'great work to do this day'.

For years the nightcap was owned by the Blackburn family who kept several Charles I relics. From them, it was passed on to the Reverend G.J. Erye who gave the nightcap to Queen Victoria, who then donated it to the museum in 1899, a year after it was founded. It is made of linen and decorated with whitework embroidery, drawn-thread work, and cutwork with needle lace inserts.

Sponsored by Chris Broom

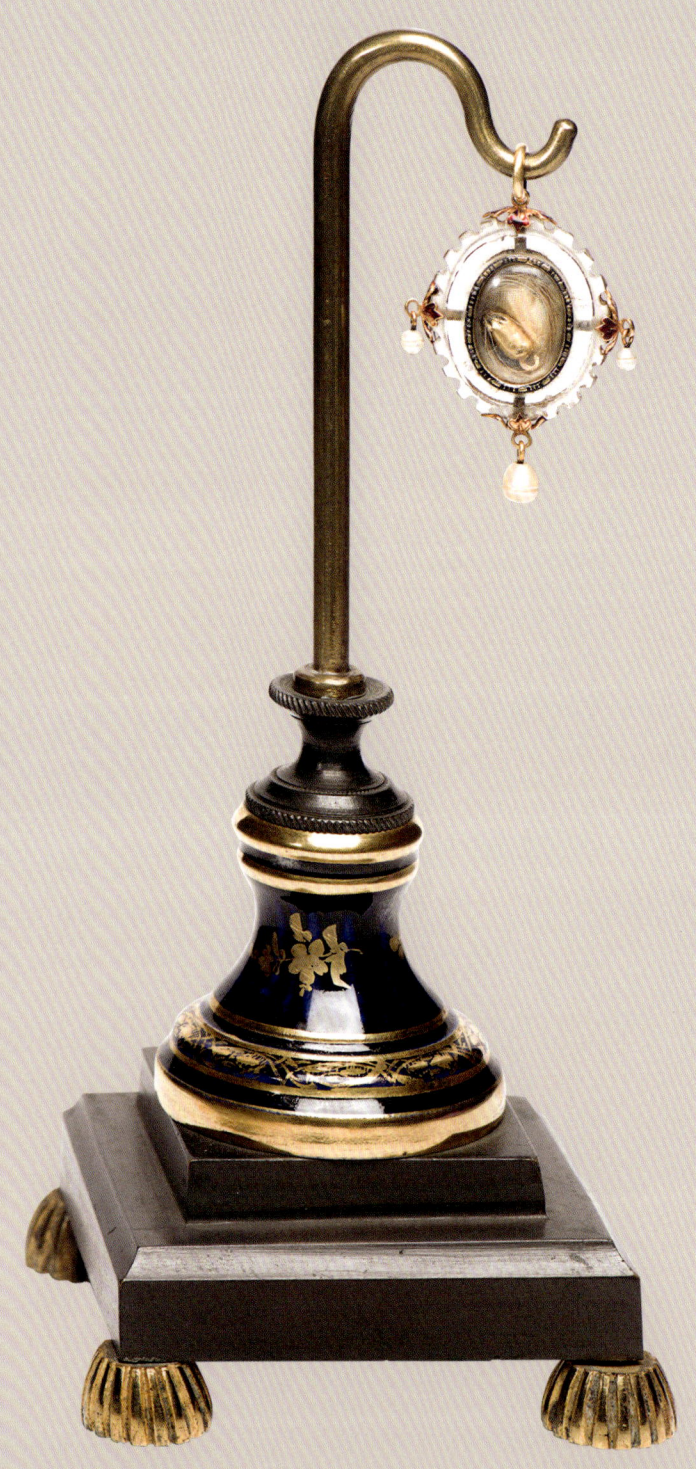

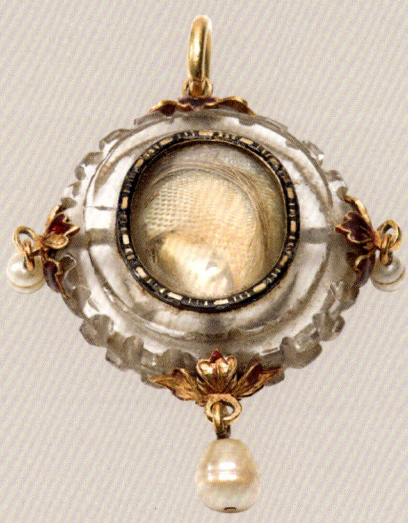

Locket containing hair of Charles I

INETCC: 1985.3021

Given by Queen Victoria

This locket, containing some of Charles I's hair, was given to the museum by Queen Victoria. An inscription attests that it was presented to her in 1846 by the Duke of Fitz-James, a descendant of an illegitimate son of James II (son of Charles I) and the Marquess of Hertford, a descendant of a Royalist commander during the Civil War, who attended the King at the Treaty of Newport and played a crucial role in organising his burial.

Soon after his execution, there was a brisk trade in vials, boxes and jewellery said to contain the blood or hair of the late King. Royalists and High Anglicans began to regard Charles as a martyr, giving objects associated with him the status of holy relics. We don't know whether this hair was cut from Charles' head upon his death or whether it was taken when his body was exhumed from its tomb at St George's Chapel Windsor in 1813. This was apparently to check that his body was in the tomb, but it was also examined by Sir Henry Halford, Physician to the King, and several pieces of hair were removed and encased in jewellery.

Sponsored by Caroline Hannam

The Royal Prisoners by C.W. Cope, 1855

NETCC: P.1986.2082
Given by A. Caultauld, 1952

Two of Charles I's children, Princess Elizabeth and Prince Henry, were imprisoned at Carisbrooke after their father's execution. Elizabeth soon fell ill and died at the age of only 14. In this painting, Henry and a guard discover the body of the dead princess.

From a young age, Elizabeth demonstrated both great academic ability and spiritual sensitivity. Her keen interest in Bible study and her mastery of its two original languages, Hebrew and Greek, was renowned. Her father called her 'Temperance' because of her calm and patient character.

The artist Charles West Cope (1811-1890) uses many symbolic details to illustrate the story of her life and emphasise the tragic nature of her death. The books on the floor allude to her intellect and passion for learning, while the lute suggests her musical ability. An open Bible positioned beneath her head illustrates her piety, and an open bird-cage symbolises her spirit liberated from imprisonment as she clasps a miniature portrait of her late father.

Sponsored by Phoebe Jane Smith (née Stark)

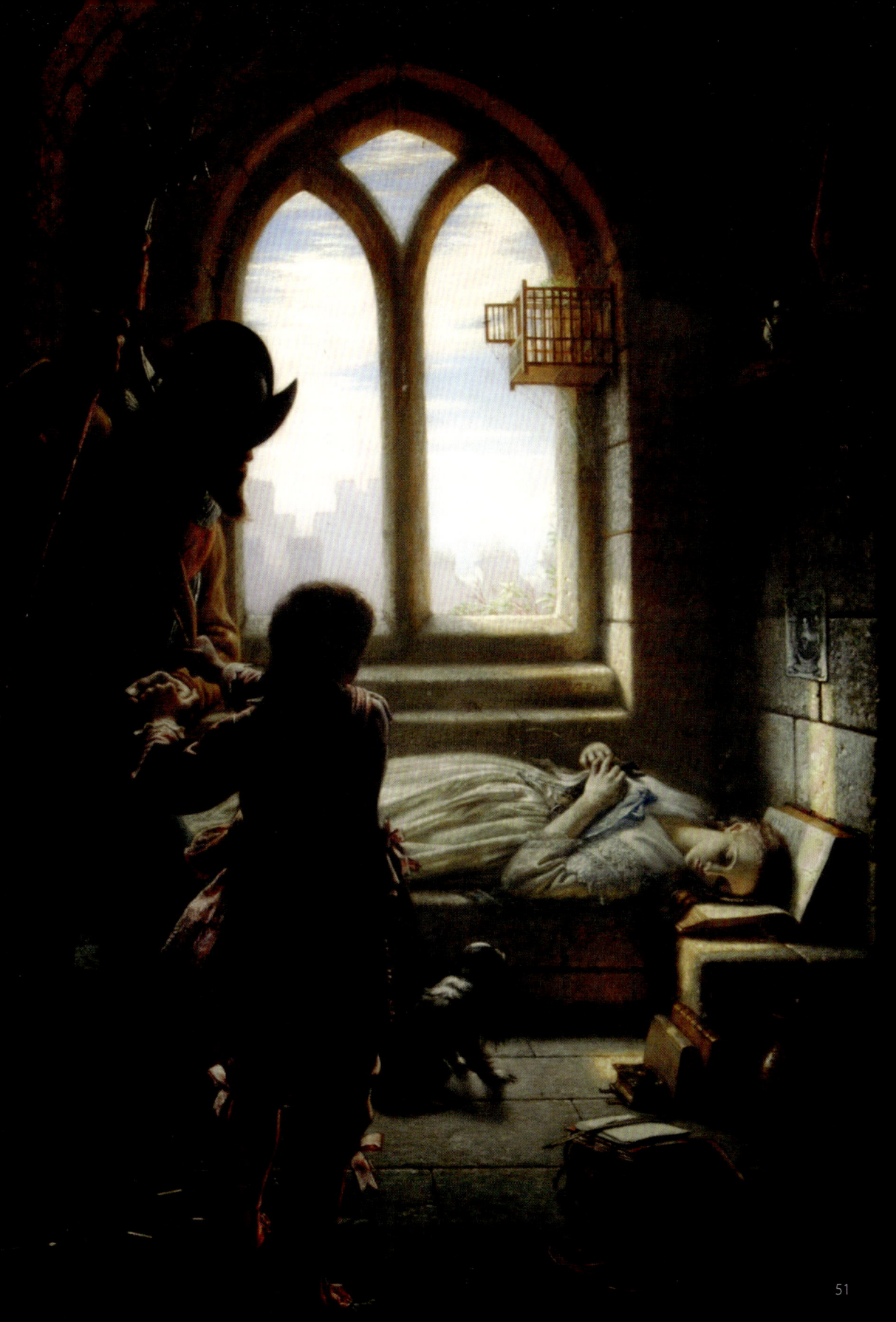

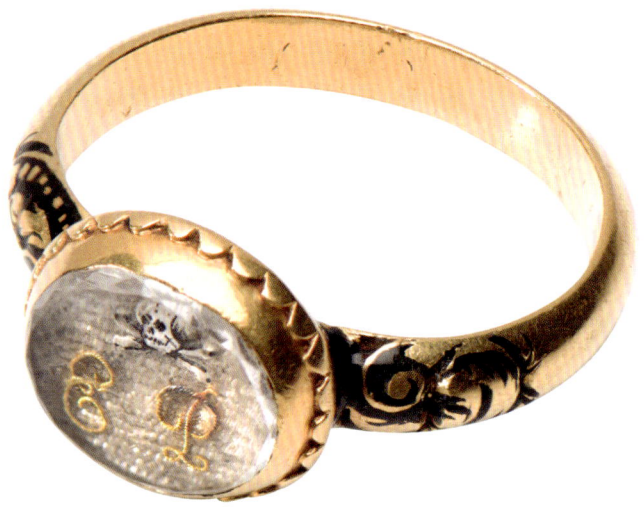

Ring containing a fragment of Princess Elizabeth's dress

NETCC: 1985.3015
Given by Princess Beatrice

Just a few days after Princess Elizabeth arrived at Carisbrooke, she was caught in a rain shower while on the bowling green. She had been frail throughout her childhood, and already weakened by illness and grief at her father's execution, she fell seriously ill. Elizabeth died, probably from consumption (tuberculosis), on September 8th, 1650.

Mementoes of the Princess were kept at the time of her death and were highly valued. She was regarded as a martyr like her father. This ring was probably made in the seventeenth century and contains a fragment of the dress in which she died in. It is decorated with a skull and crossed bones and the letters EP.

Sponsored for Edward Connoley

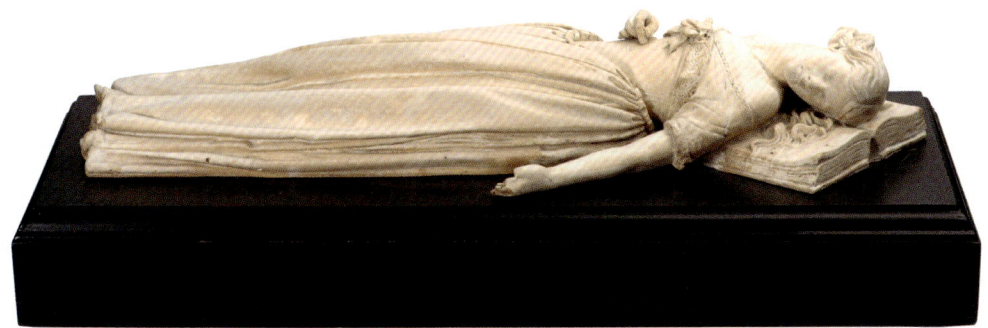

Maquette for a monument to Princess Elizabeth

NETCC: 1985.5110
Given by Princess Beatrice, 1923

When the new St. Thomas's Church, Newport, was being built in 1854, Queen Victoria decided that there should be a fitting memorial to the young Princess who was buried there. Italian-born Baron Carlo Marochetti (1805-1867), the Queen's favourite sculptor, was commissioned to do the work.

This maquette, a pattern for the full-size sculpture, was presented to Victoria for her approval and was later kept in her home at Osborne House. The model for Elizabeth's face was a young Julia Jackson, the niece and favourite subject of pioneering photographer, Julia Margaret Cameron. According to tradition, Elizabeth is said to have died holding or resting her head on the bible given to her by her father. The effigy remains in the church, now known as Newport Minster.

Sponsored by The Trustees of Carisbrooke Castle Museum

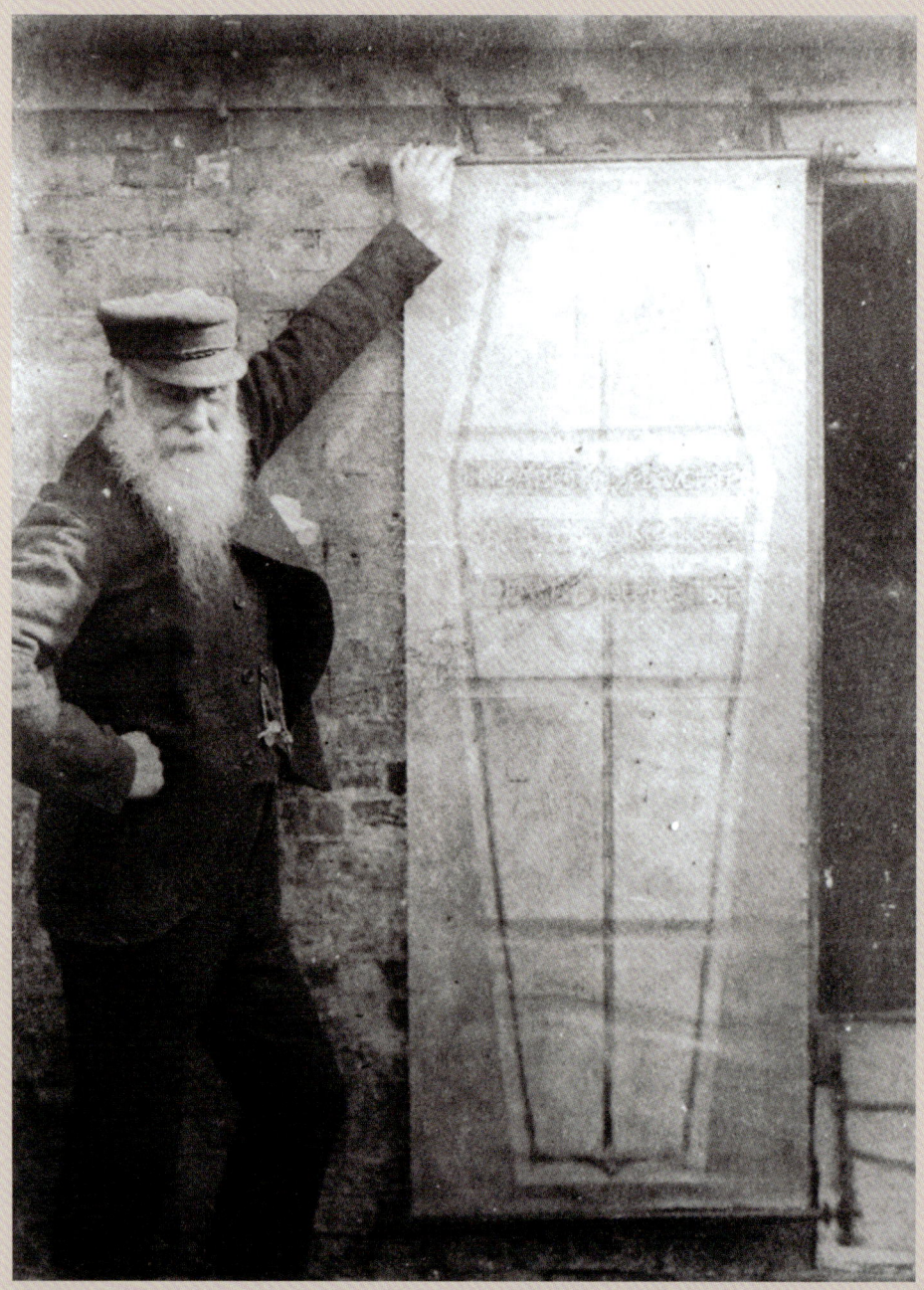

William Leddicott of the Olde Curiosity Shop with a rubbing of Elizabeth's coffin
NETCC: 1990.248

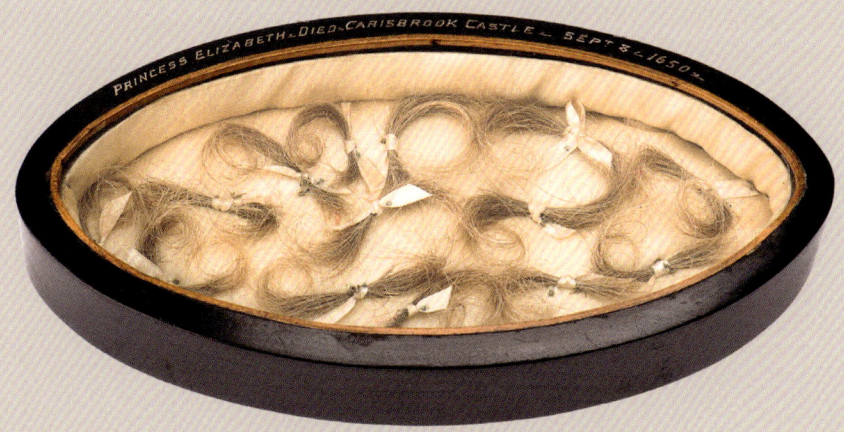

Locks of Princess Elizabeth's hair

NETCC: 1985.4857
Given by Princess Beatrice

When Elizabeth died at 14 years old, she had been a prisoner of parliament since she was just six years old. Her body was buried with little ceremony in St Thomas's Church, Newport. Its unmarked location was forgotten until her coffin was rediscovered by workmen lifting the floor in 1793.

When the church was rebuilt 60 years later, her coffin was exhumed, and a secret examination of the contents was performed. Dr Ernest P. Wilkins, a local doctor who was later the curator of the Isle of Wight Museum, published his findings in a pamphlet (which was suppressed by the town council) and took several 'souvenirs' including these locks of hair.

Some years later, William Ledicott, the owner of 'the Olde Curiosity Shoppe' in Newport, was rebuked by the Home Office for displaying in his shop window a rib bone and some hair. He was eventually persuaded to give the items to Queen Victoria who had the rib bone reinterred and donated the hair to the Museum.

Sponsored by Dide Bedford

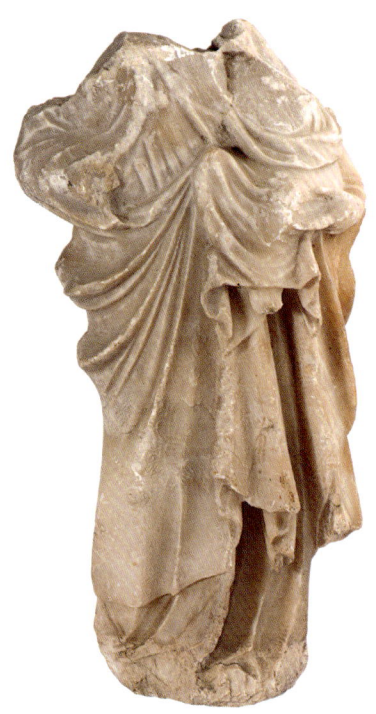

Alabaster statue of Virgin and child

NETCC: 1985.4790
Transferred from the old Newport Museum, given by Edward Wilkins

Incredibly, this fifteenth-century statue of the Virgin Mary and infant Jesus was dug up in Newport High Street in 1828. We'll never know if it was deliberately buried, discarded, or accidentally lost there – it may possibly have come from the nearby St Thomas's Church. At some point in its history both figures have lost their heads, perhaps by accident, or maybe the statue was vandalised during the Reformation of the sixteenth century. At this time many religious images were broken or defaced in a rejection of Catholic religious practices.

The surface of the figures' draped clothing is intricately carved with fine patterns and it's likely the statue was originally polychrome – painted in bright, life-like colours. As tastes changed, many polychromed medieval sculptures were stripped of this paint, revealing the white stone underneath.

Sponsored by Sally Grylls in memory of her late sister, Mary Rose Myrtle - Kings Own Scottish Borderers Regiment.

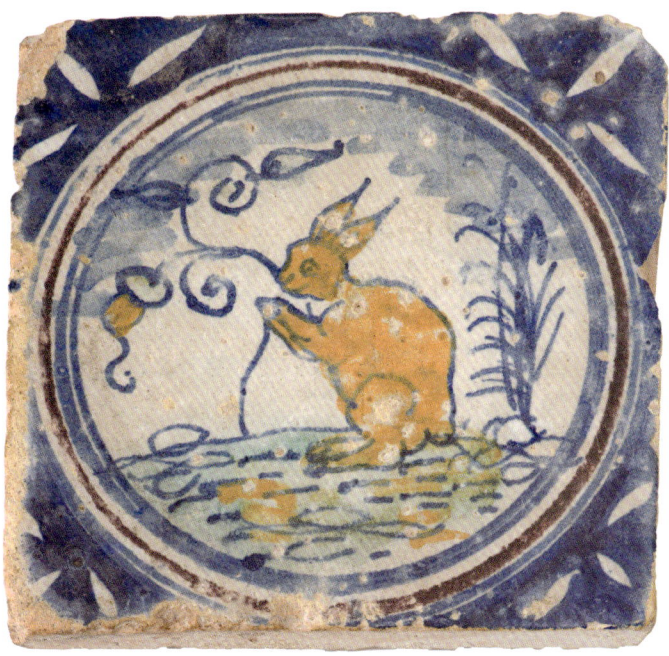

Decorated tile from the old St Thomas's Church

NETCC: 1985.4097
Transferred from the old Newport Museum, 1911

When the medieval church of St Thomas's in Newport, was demolished to make way for a new church, started in 1854, a number of its fixtures, fittings and architectural elements were recovered and collected by the old Newport Museum. Commonly known as 'delftware', this type of tin-glazed earthenware tile is of a type that originated in Italy but was later made across the Netherlands and Britain.

This example is thought to be Flemish or possibly French. The expense of installing imported ceramic tiles restricted their use to high-status buildings such as churches and the homes of the wealthy. Its polychrome (meaning several colours) decoration helps date it to no later than 1625 after which blue and white tiles became the dominant style.

Sponsored by Helen J Williams

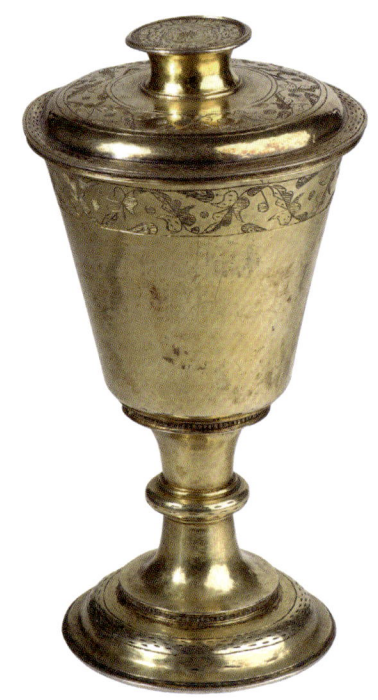

Elizabethan communion cup

NETCC: 2000.48 L
Lent by All Saints Church, Godshill

When Henry VIII ordered the dissolution of the monasteries in the 1530s, most English ecclesiastical silver was confiscated, and much of it was destroyed. However, from about 1560 when the Protestant church was firmly established under the reign of Elizabeth I, each parish church was given a new communion cup, which was to be used by the whole congregation.

Protestants rejected the Catholic belief in 'transubstantiation' (the literal transformation of bread and wine into the body and blood of Christ during the Mass) and all worshipers instead took an active part in a shared, symbolic, communion service. This cup and paten (lid) from All Saints Church in Godshill are typical of the period and may have been made from pre-Reformation silver. Its simple incised decoration would have been suitably 'decent' for Protestant tastes.

Sponsored for Ventnor and District Local History Society

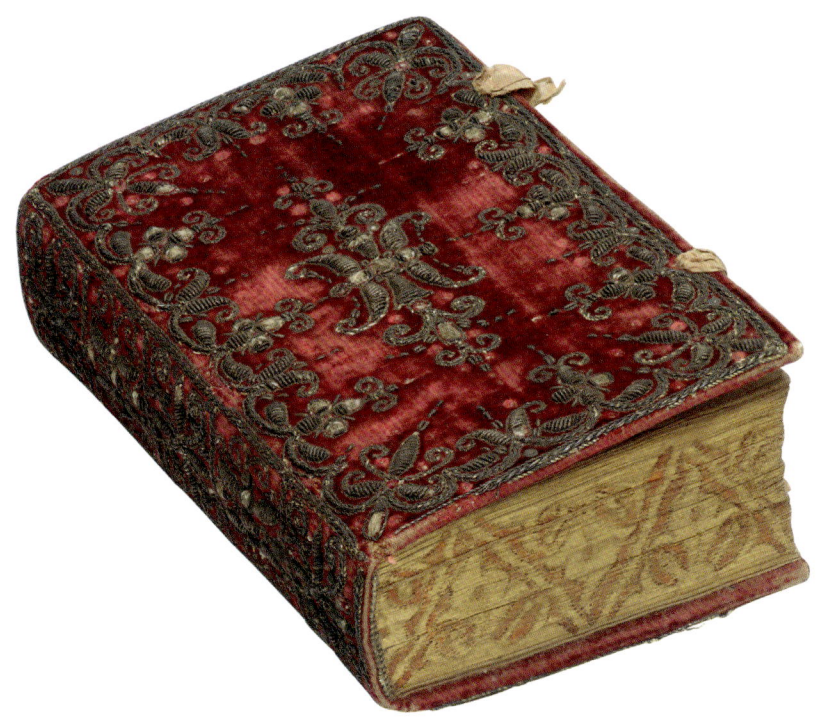

Bible and prayer book

NETCC: 2008.50

This sumptuously decorated bible and prayer book dates from 1634. At this time books were often prized possessions and bibles were given particular reverence. The richly coloured velvet and finely embroidered binding demonstrate the status of not only the book but also its wealthy owner.

The book is dedicated to Margaret Ley, the daughter of Sir James Ley (1552–1629), Lord High Treasurer (1622), and Lord President of the Council (1628). She was married to Captain John Hopson, and they lived at Ningwood House in Shalfleet, where they were frequently visited by the poet John Milton who dedicated a sonnet to her.

Sponsored for The Isle of Wight Literary Festival

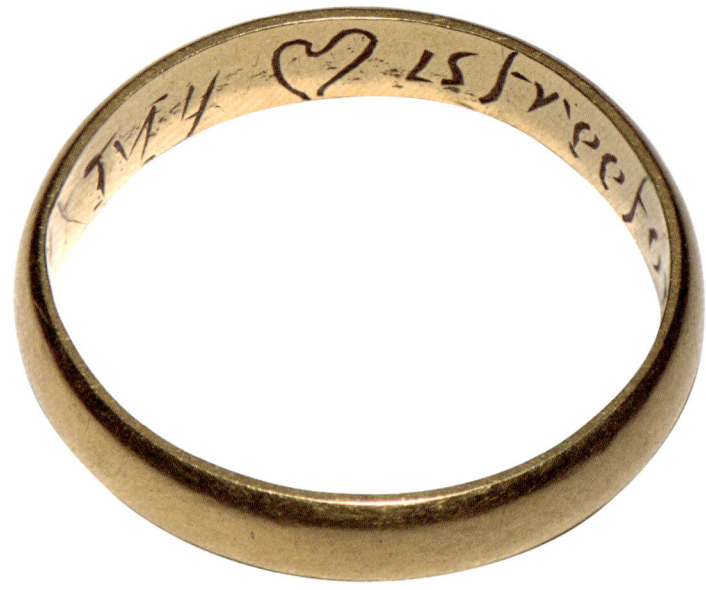

Gold posy ring

NETCC: 1985.3005
Given by Mary J. Wilson, 1927

Taking their name from the French word poésie meaning poetry, posy rings are called so because of the short sayings engraved on their surface. This ring has the inscription "My ♥ is free for God and thee" engraved on the inside of the ring - it was believed that having the words against the skin increased their power or significance. This was the wedding band of Mary Shutler who married Henry Devenish at St Swithin's Church in Thorley on January 26th, 1737. Henry owned many properties on the Isle of Wight and the couple and many of their descendants are buried in the small graveyard surrounding the old St Swithin's Church.

Sponsored by C M Tiley

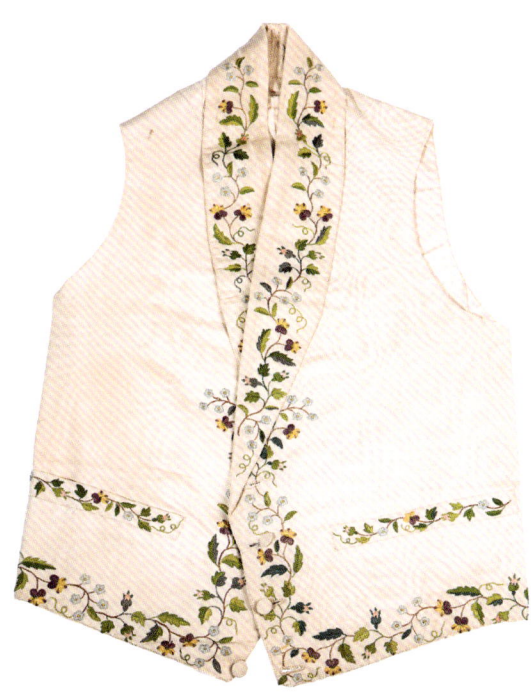

Georgian wedding waistcoat

NETCC: 1985.3389
Given by Mrs A Hearn, 1959

This exquisite waistcoat was worn during a wedding ceremony held at Arreton Church in 1820. It is made from watered silk and is decorated with hand-embroidered pansies and forget-me-nots. These flowers were chosen well for a wedding as they symbolised loving thought and loyalty. In the Georgian period, waistcoats could be one of the more colourful and elaborate parts of a man's wardrobe and were used particularly for special occasions. When it was given to the museum in the 1950s, the donor noted it had been embroidered by the 'young ladies of Hasley Manor.'

Sponsored by Harriet Robinson

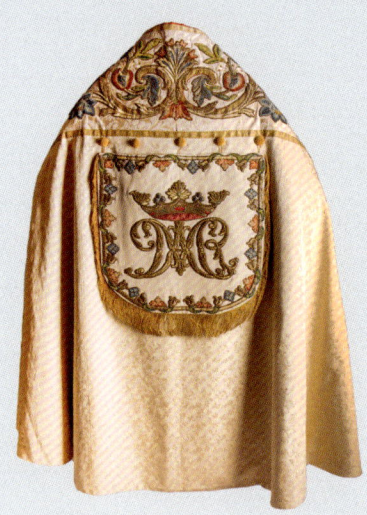

St Dominic's Vestment

NETCC: 1990.107 L
Lent by the Catholic Diocese of Portsmouth

This richly decorated cope (a cloak worn by members of the clergy) incorporates embroidery dating from the 1660s. It was made by nuns who lived in a Belgian community founded by Father Philip Thomas Howard for English Roman Catholic women who wanted to become nuns at a time when monasteries and nunneries were still prohibited in England. In 1794, as French Revolutionary forces advanced, the nuns were forced to flee and arrived in England as refugees. As they escaped, they buried the embroidery in Brussels for safekeeping and reclaimed it two years later. They finally settled at Carisbrooke in 1866 in a priory built for them by the Dowager Countess of Clare. The embroidery was restored and remounted in 1940 by Sister Mary Hyacinth Graham.

The enclosed community who lived at St Dominic's were nuns of the Order of Preachers, founded in the thirteenth century by the Spanish Saint Dominic Guzman. Their skilled creation and conservation of the order's vestments have given us fine examples of beautifully made textiles and embroidery. The nuns were the last community of Dominican nuns in Britain and the priory closed in 1989.

Sponsored by Veronica Hattersley

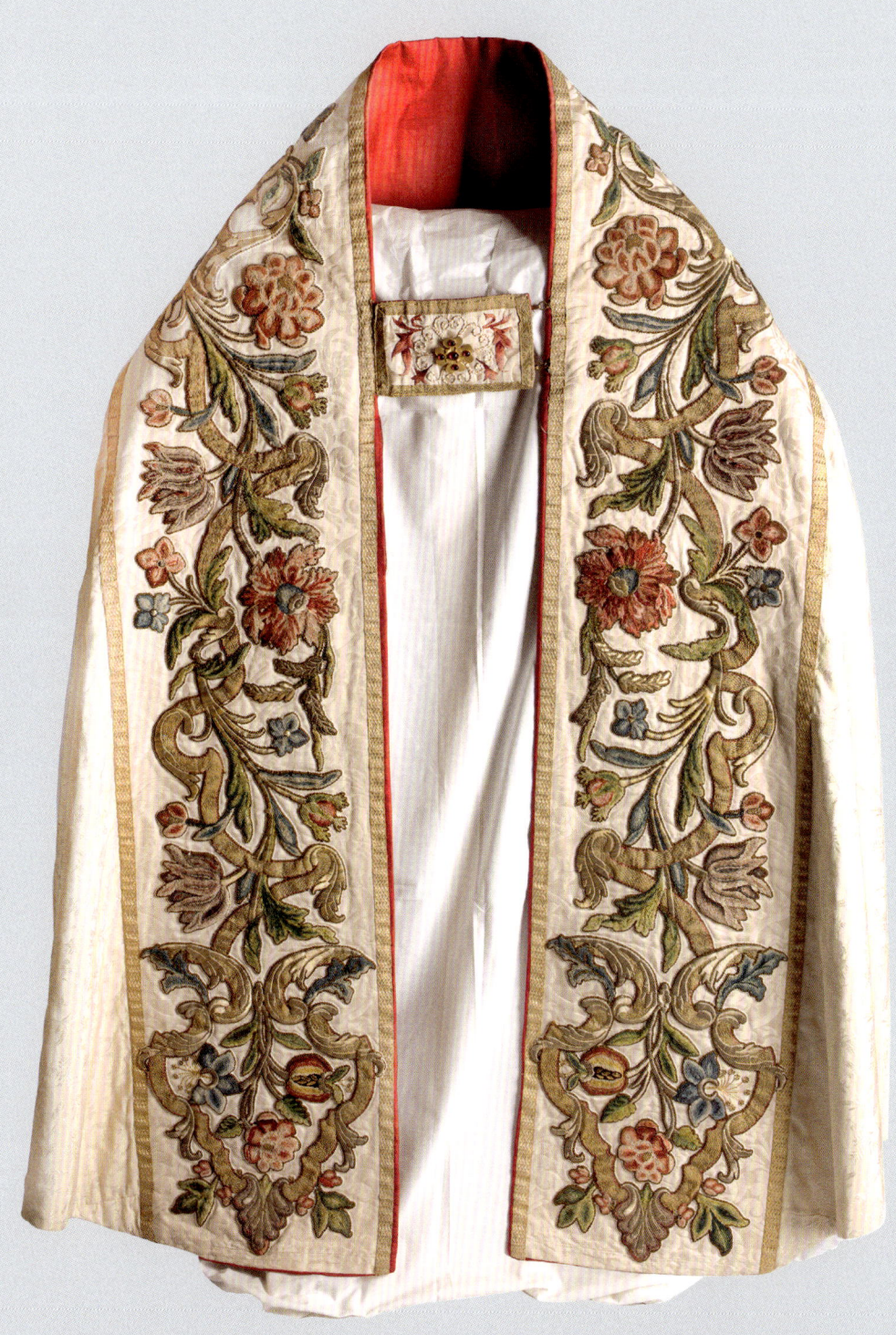

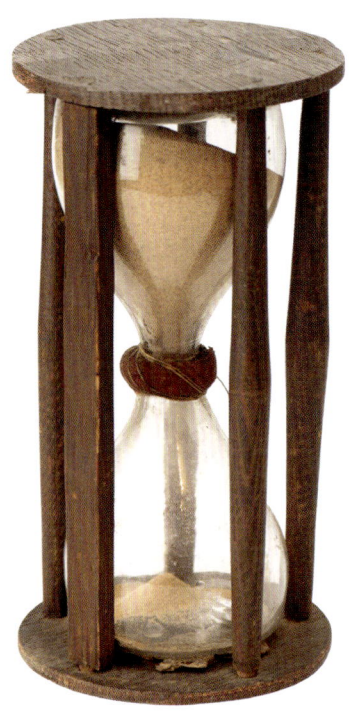

Walter Caws' sermon timer

NETCC: 2022.79
Given by Claire Nobbs in memory of Brian Graham Nobbs, 2022

Walter Deakin Caws (1836-1913) was a carpenter and lay preacher on the Isle of Wight during the nineteenth century. Born in Seaview, Walter was apprenticed at age 15 and worked as a carpenter and joiner on the Island for the rest of his life. He was a Bible Christian, a Methodist denomination, and on Sundays would travel around preaching in the Island's Methodist and Bible Christian chapels using this hourglass to time his sermons.

Walter recorded each of his sermons from 1879 to 1912 in a notebook, detailing which bible verses he based his readings on to avoid repeating sermons to the same congregation. Later he started adding extra information such as the weather and which kind member of the congregation gave him lunch. In 1901 he also records the death of his wife after a three-year-long illness. He writes: "She has done much the largest share of entering the texts I have preached from in this and other books and now I open the book once more and Oh! How I miss her."

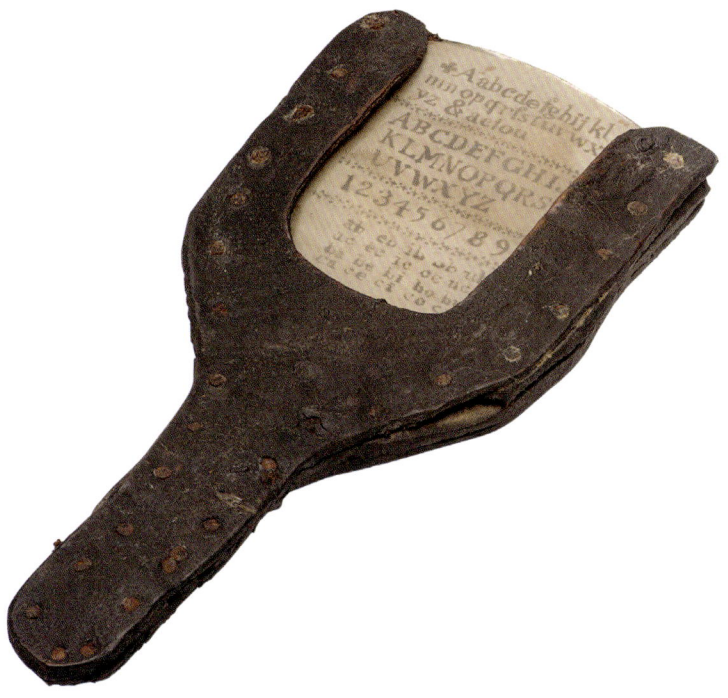

Tudor hornbook

NETCC: 1985.2964
Bequeathed by F.G. Poole, 1957

In the Tudor period, hornbooks were used to teach children the basics of the English language. A single sheet of either vellum or paper was covered with a thin layer of protective horn and placed within a holder incorporating a handle to make it easy for young children to hold. The holders were often made of wood, but this is a rare leather example. The writing shows the alphabet in upper and lower case, numbers, and common vowel combinations. Basic hornbooks like this played an important role in the education of Tudor children and ensured that expensive paper and vellum were protected while being used by young children.

Sponsored by Diane York

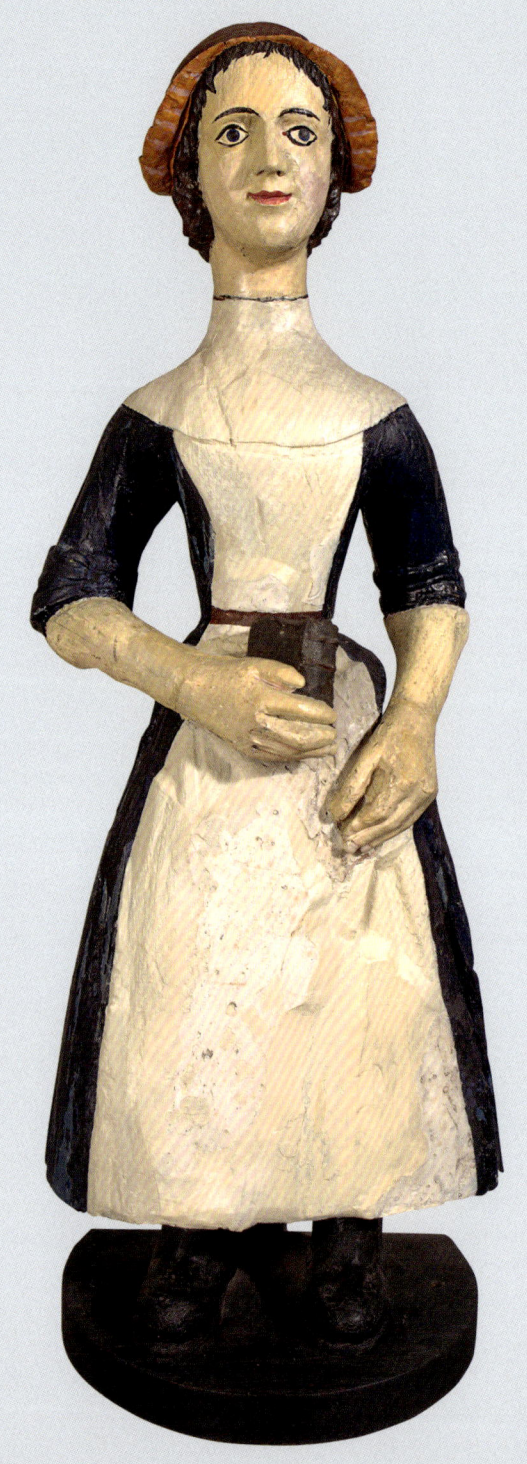

Blue Jenny

NETCC: 1985.4840

This carved wooden figure, known as Blue Jenny, stood in a niche above the door of the Blue School in Newport. The school aimed to improve "the education, board and clothing of poor girls" and was established at 10, Lugley Street in 1761 (moving to nearby 62, Crocker Street in 1886 and operating until 1907). It was run as a charity and funded by subscribers. The school taught pupils reading, writing, arithmetic, knitting, needlework, washing and household work "so that they may become good and useful servants". After completing their education, the girls were required to enter service on the Island for a year.

The school's name came from the blue uniforms that the girls wore; blue was associated with charity and was the cheapest dye available. Jenny wears the school's uniform of a blue dress, white apron, cap, and black boots. Girls were clothed "in a manner suitable to [their] station" and were given a bible and prayer book which can be seen in the figure's right hand.

Admissions registers give an insight into school life, which appeared not to be always happy. Many girls completed their education and went into service, but others were expelled from the school; offences included theft and "impertinence and obstinacy". If the girls stayed in their first place of employment for a full year, they were rewarded with one pound, although it was not uncommon for them to leave or be dismissed before this. The register also gives details of the girls who died from infectious diseases, which occasionally swept through the school.

Sponsored by Carol Alstrom

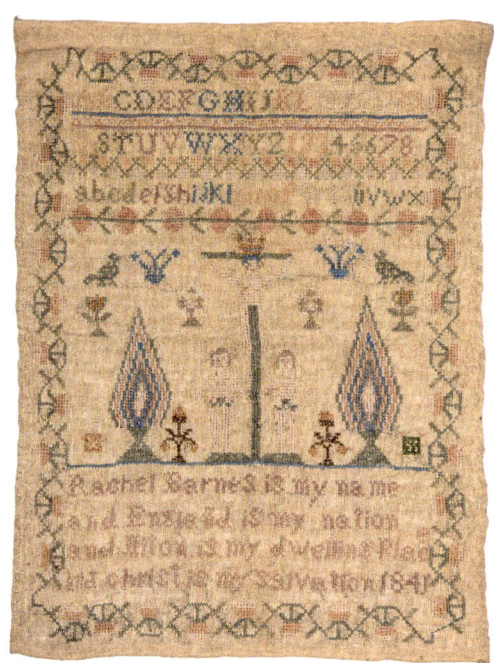

Embroidered sampler

NETCC: 1995.492
Given by M. Nicholson, 1995

Pieces of embroidery or cross stitching such as this sampler were used as a test or demonstration of skill in needlework. In the eighteenth and nineteenth centuries, young girls were taught to embroider from a young age. Poorer girls would learn these skills to enable them to embroider household linen when they went into service. For more affluent girls the ability to embroider was considered a ladylike accomplishment.

This example, stitched on linen, was made by Rachel Barnes of Niton in 1841 when she was 9 years old. She spent most of her life in service as a domestic servant, working at Dover House in Ryde. Rachel never married and by the time of the census of 1911 was living at Chale and is recorded as an 'ex-servant'. She died in 1921 at the age of 88.

Sponsored by Isle of Wight Embroiderers

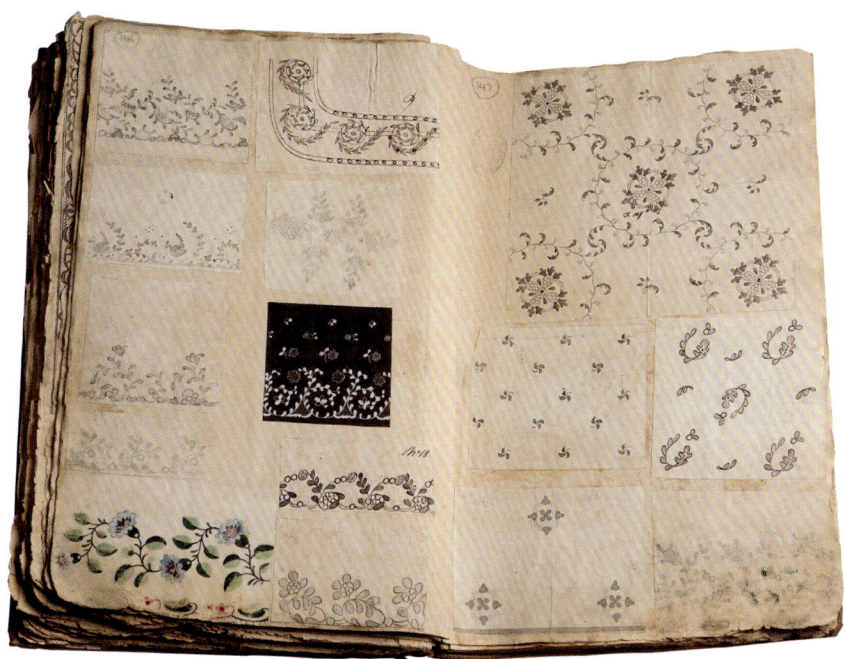

Nunn's lace factory pattern book

NETCC: 1985.3144
Transferred from the old Newport Museum, 1911

This book contains hand-drawn designs for lace made at the Nunn's factory at Broadlands on Staplers Road. For over forty years from 1827, the factory was renowned throughout Britain and Europe for the outstanding quality of the lace it produced.

In 1810 two Nottinghamshire silk stocking weavers developed a new machine for making lace. They sought investment from the father of Henry Nunn who agreed on the condition that they took his son into their partnership. Henry came to the Island in 1826, possibly attracted by the local tradition of hand lacemaking. In the 1830s, new machines and designs were developed for making 'French blond' lace, one of the finest and most desirable types. At its height, the factory made £40,000 profit a year – nearly £6 million in today's money. When Henry retired in about 1870, the factory closed dealing a serious blow to the local people it employed. The book was given by H. Shepherd, a machinist and designer at the factory.

Sponsored by Tim and Tracy Welstead

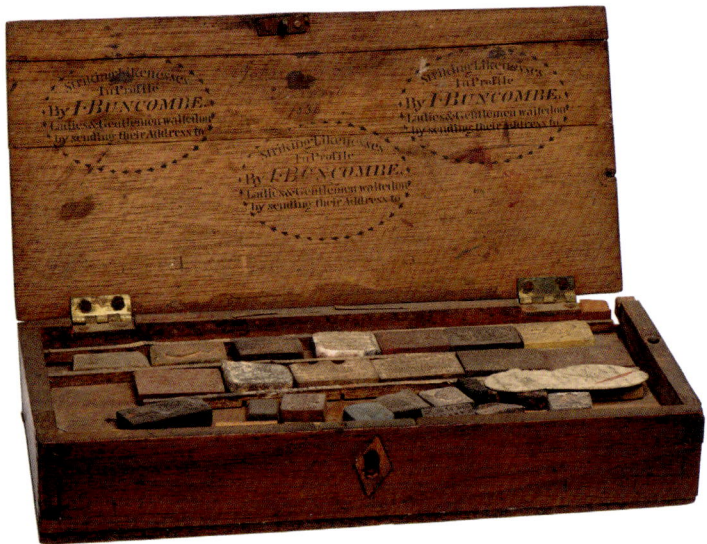

John Buncombe's paint box

NETCC: 1985.4841
Given by Bennington, 1955

John Buncombe (c.1758–1837) was a silhouette artist who lived in Newport and specialised in portraits of military men with their uniforms depicted in vibrant colours and minute attention to detail. Silhouette portraits show the outline of a person in profile and are filled with a solid colour, which is usually black. They were at their most popular during the Georgian period and because they were cheaper and quicker to make than normal portraits, they became a popular medium for a wide section of society.

During the Napoleonic War (1793-1815), thousands of troops were stationed on the Island, providing Buncombe with a plentiful supply of customers. These inexpensive portraits made attractive souvenirs to send home and Buncombe made a steady living and was able to educate his son. Despite this success, in 1828 after all his family predeceased him, apart from his young, orphaned grandchildren, Buncombe was moved to the House of Industry, the workhouse in Newport, where he died in 1837.

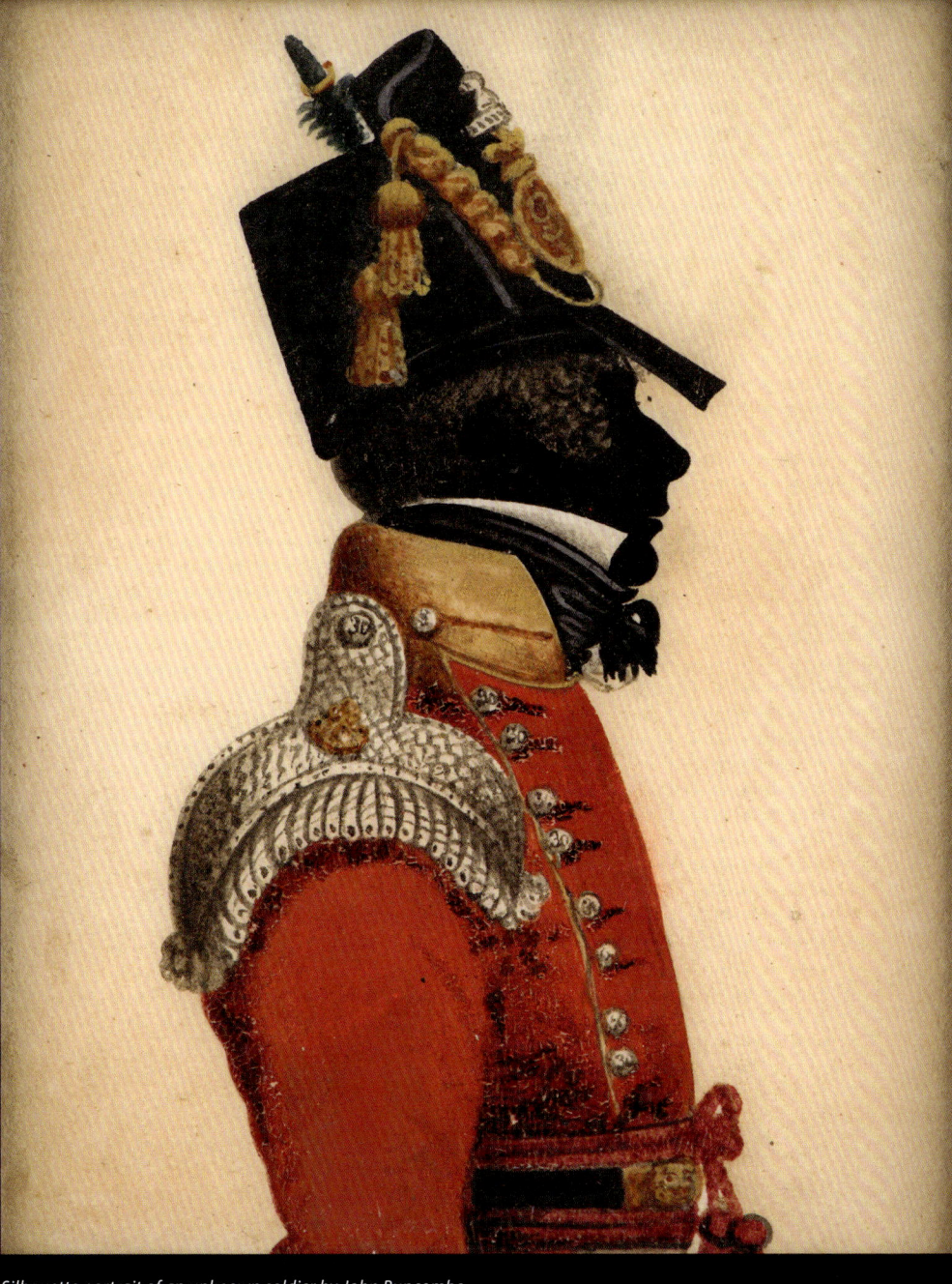

Silhouette portrait of an unknown soldier by John Buncombe
NETCC: P.986.2148

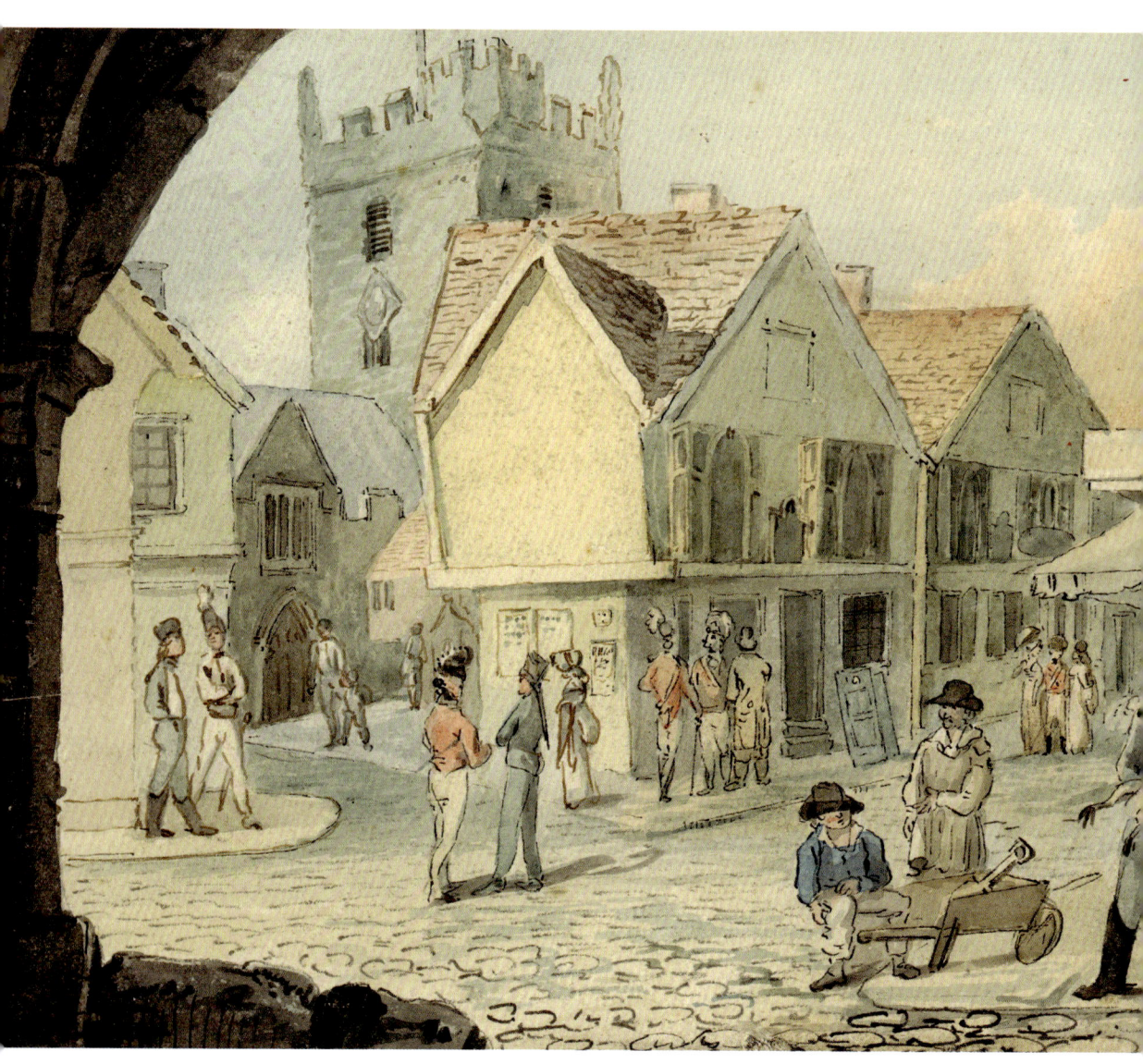

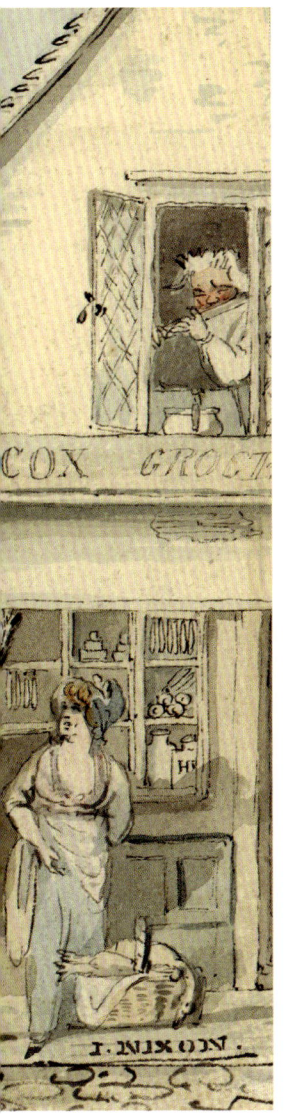

Newport High Street by John Nixon

John Nixon (1755-1818) was a London wine merchant and talented amateur artist. He travelled widely visiting Ireland, Scotland, Wales, the Isle of Man, the Netherlands and France, touring the south and west of England and visiting the Isle of Wight at least 13 times before dying at Ryde. Nixon's interests and his travels provided him with inspiration for many watercolour, pen and wash, and pencil sketches, which show his flair for both landscape and figure drawing.

Nixon was highly regarded as an artist in his own lifetime. He was an honorary exhibitor at the Royal Academy and some of his works were engraved and published. His sketches and paintings of the Island are also significant for the image they portray of the Isle of Wight two hundred years ago. This view was painted from the Butter Market underneath the arches of the seventeenth-century town hall, looking towards the twelfth-century St Thomas's Church, both buildings that were later demolished. It appears to be market day and the farmer's wife, or daughter, has been selling her geese. There are also uniformed soldiers in the street, the presence of which contributed to the Island's prosperity at this time.

NETCC: P.1986. 1556
Purchased, about 1950

Sponsored by June Hayles

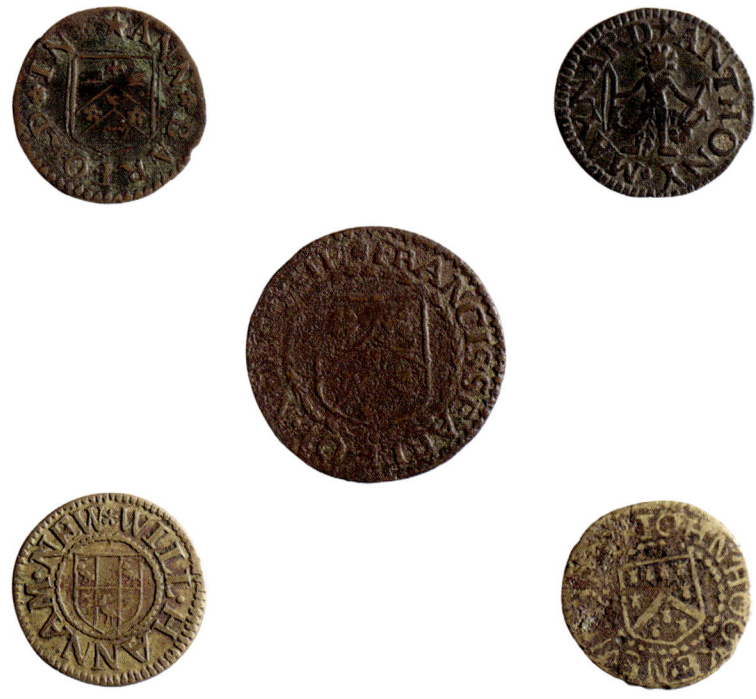

Newport trade tokens

NETCC: 1985.1131; 1985.1145; 1985.1150; 1985.1173; 1985.1186

During shortages of official currency, some businesses issued their own coins known as trade tokens. The issuing business promised to deliver its value in coin of the realm in the same way that we now use bank notes and cheques. These tokens were never officially sanctioned but were accepted and circulated widely.

These five tokens are all from seventeenth-century businesses in Newport and provide a fascinating insight into the town at this time. Most tokens show the issuer's full name or initials and indicate the type of business, either by name or by including their trade's coat of arms. Ann Barford was a stationer in Newport High Street, William Hannam a tallow chandler in Pyle Street, Anthony Maynard an apothecary in Holyrood Street, Francis Searle a brewer in Sea Street, and John Hooke (brother of scientist Robert Hooke) was a grocer in the High Street.

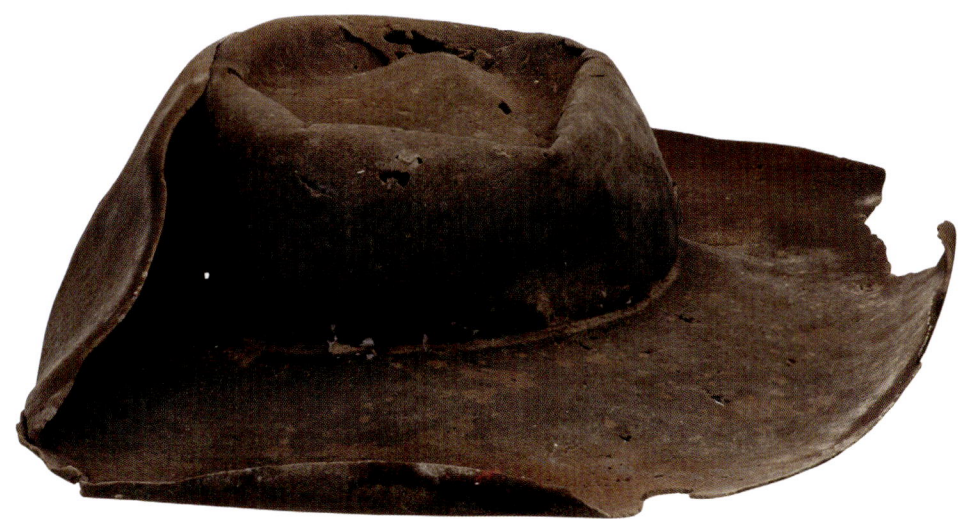

Leather hat found at the Green Dragon Inn

NETCC: 1985.3779
Given by Mr H. E. Stratton, 1924

This is a rare surviving example of an eighteenth-century man's broad-brimmed hat, found when the Green Dragon Inn was demolished to widen Town Lane in 1924. The Inn was over 300 years old and one of the oldest buildings in Newport. For centuries it was a centre for Newport social life with its large assembly room hosting lectures, theatrical productions, public meetings, and county balls. The Green Dragon tap room, which is now the site of the Prince of Wales in South Street, was particularly busy on market days that took place nearby. In 1909 the inn was inspected and closed due to a lack of customers. The inspector noted there were "six other licensed houses within a radius of 150 yards."

Sponsored by The Tony P Radio Show

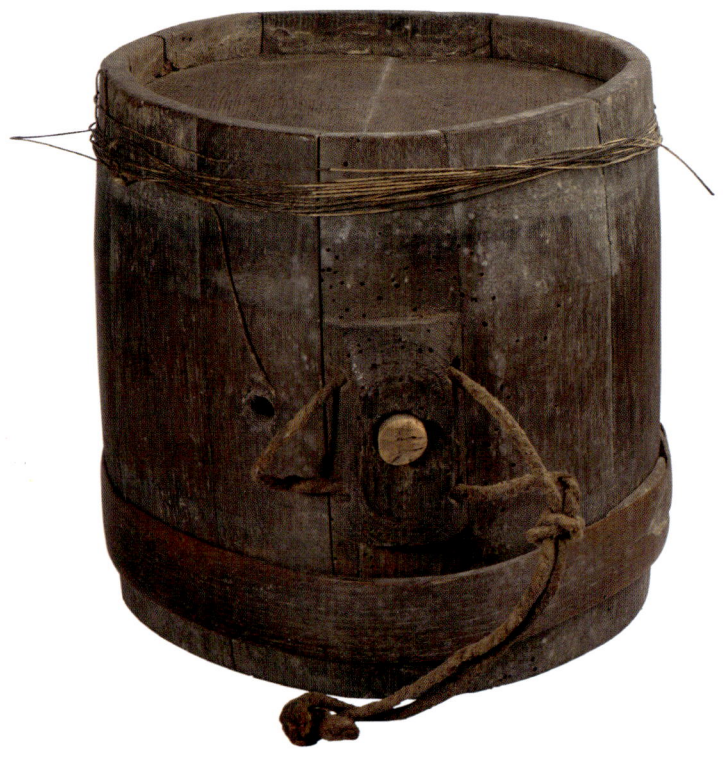

Beer firkin

NETCC: 1985.4295
Purchased, 1925

A firkin is a measurement of beer (a quarter of a barrel) and the name of the size of a cask. This firkin was used at Marvell Farm, near Blackwater, in the nineteenth century and would probably have contained cider or beer and would have been used to carry drink out to the farm's labourers. At this time, most agricultural work was manual and intensive. During the summer workers needed to not only drink plenty of fluids but also consume a lot of calories and beer and cider could provide both these things.

Sponsored by Vectis Tavern

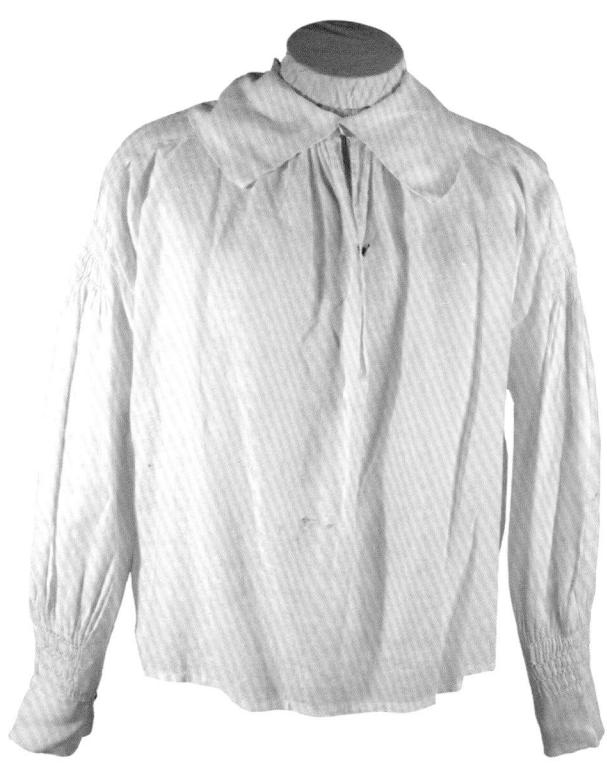

Worker's smock

NETCC: 1985.3393
Given by Mr D. Cotton, 1975

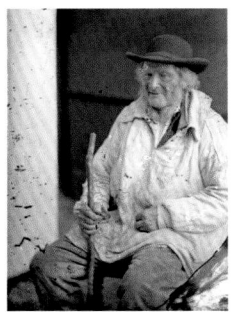

George Tullege, shepherd at Shanklin Manor Farm, wearing a smock.
NETCC: N.1986.2287

Outer garments like this were traditionally worn by the Island's rural workers, especially shepherds, throughout the eighteenth and nineteenth centuries. Often made from hard-wearing linen, smocks had ample material across the back and breast, but the sleeves were gathered with pleats held in place and decorated by smocking, a type of surface embroidery in a honeycomb pattern across the pleats, that controlled the fullness while allowing a degree of stretch. This made the smock a form-fitting but flexible work garment and protected the clothes worn underneath from dirt.

Sponsored for The Isle of Wight Story Festival

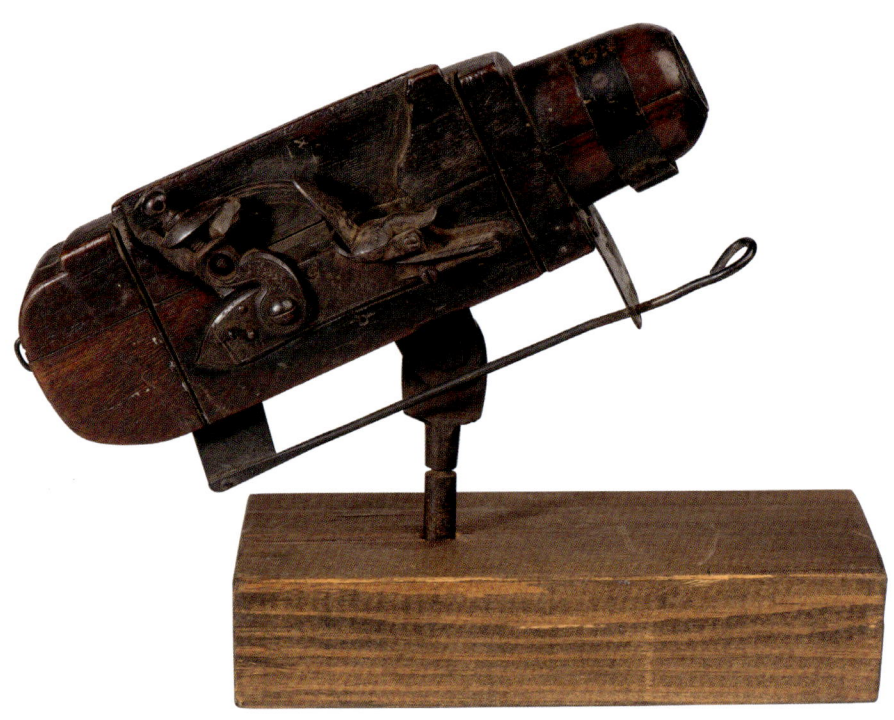

Anti-poaching spring gun

NETCC: 1985.2089

This tripwire-operated 'spring gun' or 'trap gun' would have been loaded and set in a woodland area as an anti-poaching measure. While poaching has been illegal since medieval times, historically most poachers were subsistence poachers. These were poor people who hunted animals to supplement their meagre diet. It was legally required that people were informed that these anti-poaching devices were in use, so notices were displayed, and town criers made announcements. They were sometimes loaded with stones or rock salt, which were less lethal projectiles than lead shot, but they remained a dangerous and indiscriminate weapon.

This example probably dates to the late eighteenth or early nineteenth centuries but the technology dates as far back as the early seventeenth century and was used to protect all kinds of property, sometimes even to protect cemeteries from grave robbers. The use of spring guns was banned in 1827.

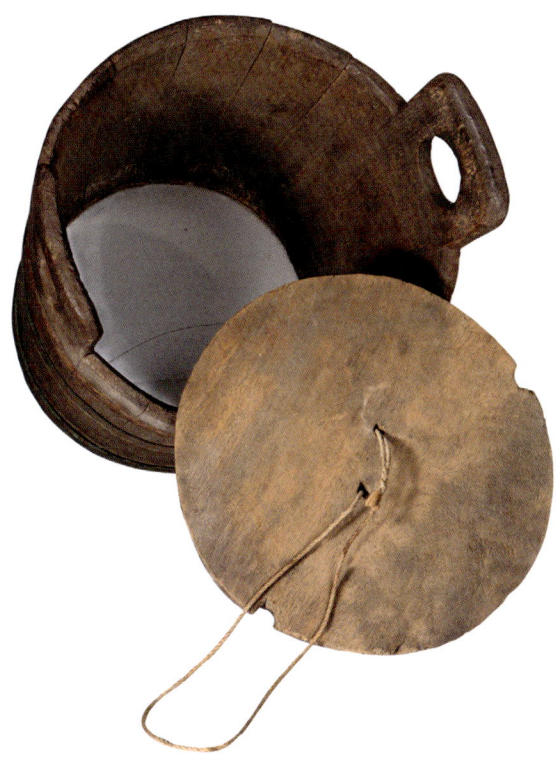

Smuggling 'peep tub'

NETCC: 1985.2104
Given by T.E. Roberts, 1954

To avoid detection, smugglers sank their contraband, strung together with rope and weighed down with lead weights. Used by Chale smugglers, this 'peep tub' with its glass bottom could be lowered into the water to see under the surface. A grapple hook was then used to grab the cargo bringing it back to the surface. Its false base allowed the tub to be used as an ordinary bucket so as not to raise suspicion.

Smuggling paid well and poor farm labourers and fishermen were glad of the money, although it was dangerous work with the threat of violence and arrest ever-present. The high import duties on goods such as spirits, tea and tobacco were loathed by most, and so-called 'free-traders' had the sympathy of many Islanders. It is estimated that at its most widespread, 8 out of 10 Islanders were involved in the illegal trade in some way.

Sponsored by Adam Provis

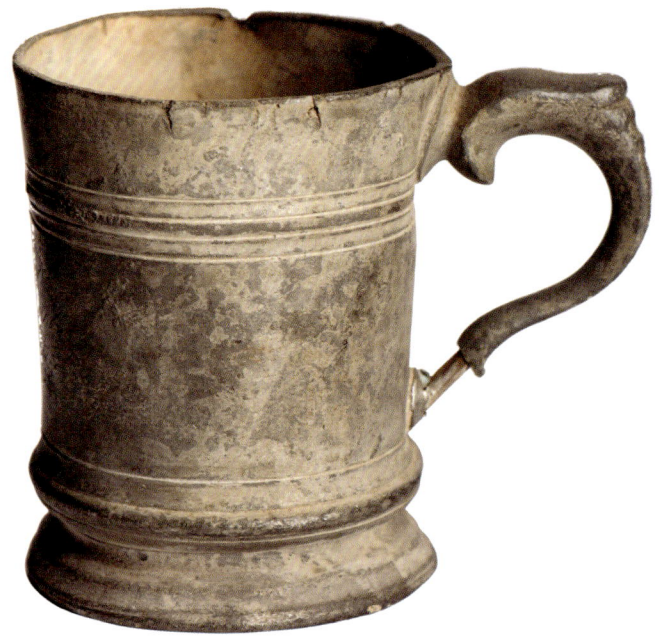

Pewter tankard

NETCC: 1985.4270

This pewter tankard was used at the Castle and Banner Pub in Newport, probably in the early nineteenth century, and is engraved with the name G. Poulter. Tankards became popular drinking vessels in the mid-seventeenth century and pewter, sometimes known as 'poor man's silver' because of how it shined when polished, was a common material. Unlike pottery, pewter doesn't break if dropped and is easy to reshape if it becomes dented or deformed, making it particularly suited for use in pubs.

The Castle and Banner on Hunnyhill dated back to at least the eighteenth century and there was a pub on the site until it closed in the 1980s. G. Poulter whose name is engraved on the side of the tankard may have been the publican or a regular drinker at the pub.

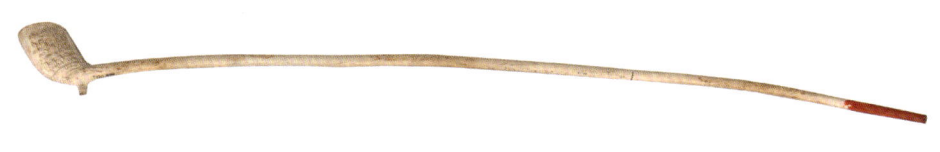

Churchwarden's clay pipe, made by Robert Cole

NETCC: 1985.2711
Given by the Misses Read, 1922

The Isle of Wight is one of the only places in Britain where clay suitable for pipe making can be found. There was a pipe manufacturer in Orchard Street, Newport, throughout the nineteenth century and until at least 1911. This pipe has a bowl decorated with a rose, a thistle and a shamrock design and includes the name of its maker, Robert Cole, who ran the Orchard Street business from around 1839, when he was 22, until the 1880s.

This style of pipe with a very long stem is known as a 'churchwarden's pipe, supposedly because this long stem allowed the bowl of the pipe to be placed out of a window, enabling churchwardens to smoke in church. However, the real benefit of such a pipe seems to have been that the long stem produced a cooler smoke due to the distance it travelled from the bowl and kept the smoke away from the user's eyes. In Germany, they are known as 'reading pipes'.

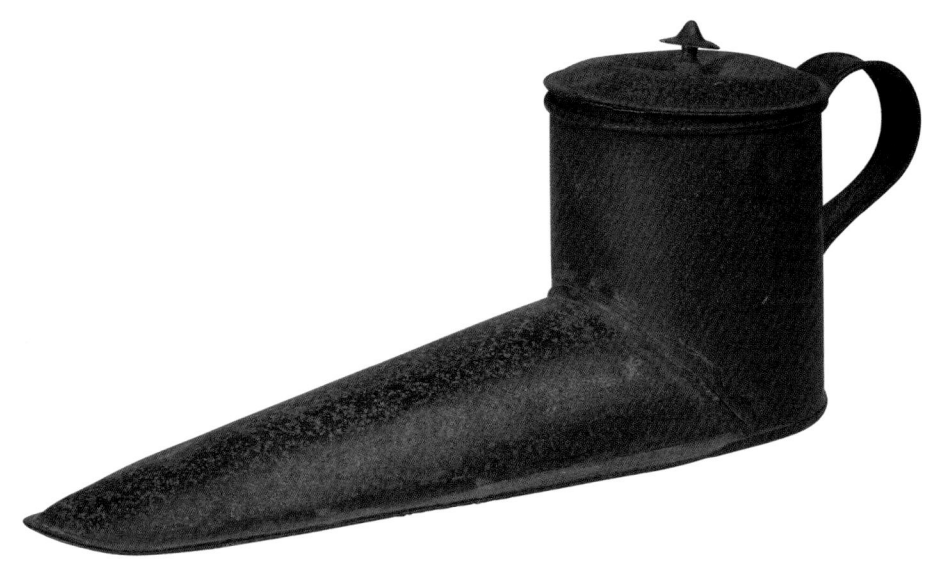

Ale muller

NETCC: 1985.2337

Given by Rev. L.T.S. Sims Williams, 1965

This iron 'shoe' muller would have been filled with ale and then its toe would be placed into the hot coals of an open fire. Warmed ale, sometimes mulled with spices such as nutmeg, a measure of brandy or rum and sugar and known as 'flip', was a popular winter drink. Many people also believed that ale was healthier when drunk warm. Cone-shaped mullers were also used but perhaps the most common method of warming ale was plunging a red-hot iron rod, known as a loggerhead and original designed for melting pitch on ships, directly into the liquid.

Sponsored for Boojum And Snark

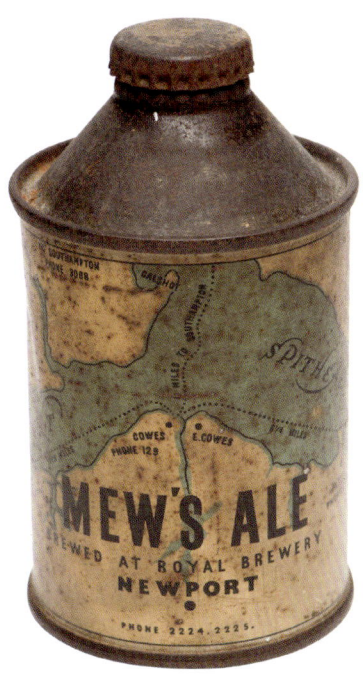

Tin of Mew's Ale

NETCC: 2017.7

Given by Gwyneth Dawson, 2014

Founded in the late eighteenth century by two brothers, Mews and Co. Brewers had breweries in Newport and Lymington and owned several local pubs. The business prospered with a significant part of its trade coming from supplying army canteens. In 1850 they were granted a royal warrant to supply Queen Victoria when she was in residence at Osborne House, renaming their Newport brewery the 'Royal Brewery'.

When Walter Langton joined the business in the 1880s it was renamed Mew Langton & Co and by the 1890s, they were using modern methods of 'pneumatic malting'. They continued to innovate and in the 1930s were one of a small number of British brewers to start producing canned beer. This style of can was known as a 'cone-top' and was easier to transport than heavy and fragile glass bottles. It was brewed at the Royal Brewery and its label shows the business's extensive network of breweries and distributors.

Sponsored for Style Of Wight Magazine

1784

February the 26 on Thursday Night at 2 o Clock the Independance a large Ship from Baltimore come to London lode with Tobacco and Staves was lost upon the Mexton at Atherfild Rocks the Crew was forced to Remain upon part of the wreck until Friday Morning the 27 of which one Black boy Perished the rest and Part the Marchent and Several others of the Crew Nerily Escaped the Ship and most part Cargo lost

1784

June the 15 on Tuesday Morning at 1 o Clock a Ship Named the Twine Ship Burdned 250 tuns from Vergina Bound to London lode with Tobacco and Staves was lost upon the Mexton at Atherfild Rocks the Ship and most part of the Cargo lost
Crew Saved

1784

Thursday November the 11 at 8 o Clock at Night a Brig from Madria bound to Denmarke lode with Osiers Run ashore at Chilton Chine the Ship and Cargo was Saved

1784

Monday November the 15 at 3 o Clock in the Morning a English Cutter from Malaga lode with fruit bound to London was cast a Shore at Sudmore Point Burdned about 10 tuns the Cutter and most part of the Cargo was lost Crew Saved

1785

January the 5 on Wednsday Morning Dutch Brig from St Ubes bound to lode with Salt was lost under Clift of Wight the Ship and Cargo lost

1785

January the 6 on Thursday at 11 o Clock English Ship from Portugal bound to had Some Dollars Run a Shore in a the Ship and Cargo Saved

1785

January the 8 on Saturday Night at Hoy from St Ubes bound to Holan a Shore at Hawks lege a little to the Chine her Cargo was all lost the hoy after a great deal of Work

1785

January the 30 on Sunday Night at a large Ship from Vergina bound the Master of her lode with Tobacco and Turpentine the Mexton at Atherfild Rocks the of the Cargo was lost Burdned 80

1785

August the 2 on Teusday Night the wind lighting a French Brig from Lisbon had on board Dom Cyder opposite to Park Crew Saved Ship

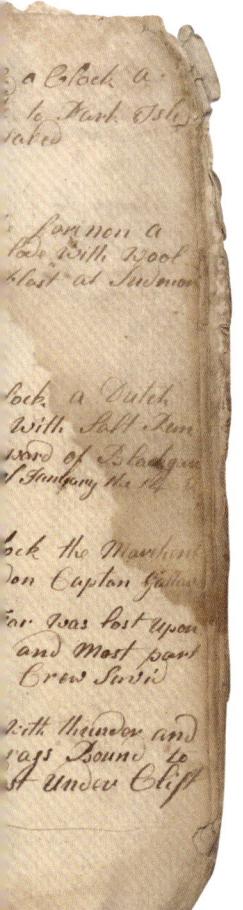

Shipwreck logbook

This rare eyewitness record of shipwrecks off the Isle of Wight was kept by James Wheeler, a longshoreman from Blackgang, between 1746 and 1808. Alongside details of the wrecks, it provides interesting information about the cargo of the ships as well as trading routes.

Over the centuries, hundreds of ships have come to grief along the Island's coast, especially along the 'Back of the Wight' (from Freshwater Bay to St Catherine's Point) with its treacherous ledges and exposure to fierce Atlantic swells. Generations of local men risked their lives crewing the lifeboats that launched rescue attempts from the villages and chines along the coast. A wreck could be a welcome addition to the income of poor fishermen and farmers, despite the threat of prosecution for theft. More legitimate work included being hired to unload cargo from wrecks and, if the ship couldn't be recovered, to break it up.

NETCC: D.1986.1

Sponsored by Stephen Holden

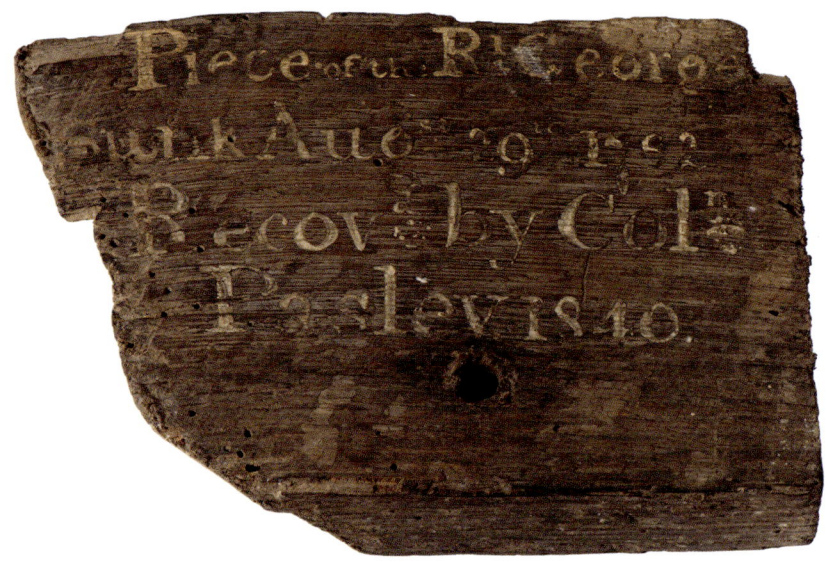

Fragment of the wreck of the Royal George

NETCC: 1985.4822

Gift from Boxell, 1964

HMS Royal George was a 100-gun first-rate ship of the line of the Royal Navy. Launched in 1756 she was the largest warship in the world. On August 29th, 1782, while anchored off Portsmouth undergoing routine maintenance work, the ship became overbalanced, filled with water and sank. On board were most of her crew as well as workmen, visiting relatives and traders. Around 900 people, including up to 300 women and 60 children, drowned. Many of the victims washed ashore at Ryde and were buried in a mass grave along the foreshore.

Over the subsequent 60 years, salvage attempts were made both to recover valuable components and because she was a major hazard to navigation. Early divers helped raise guns and break up the wreckage until it was finally destroyed in a controlled explosion in 1840. It was during one of the diving expeditions in 1834 that the site of the sunken Mary Rose was located.

Sponsored for East Cowes Heritage Centre

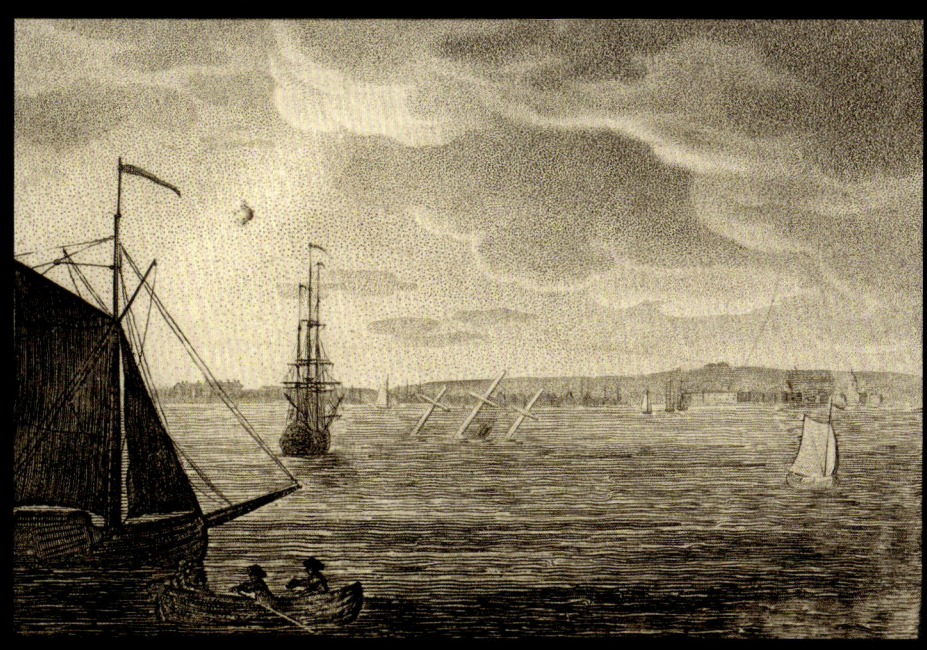

The wreck of the Royal George seen from Ryde, 1789
NETCC: P.1986.1283

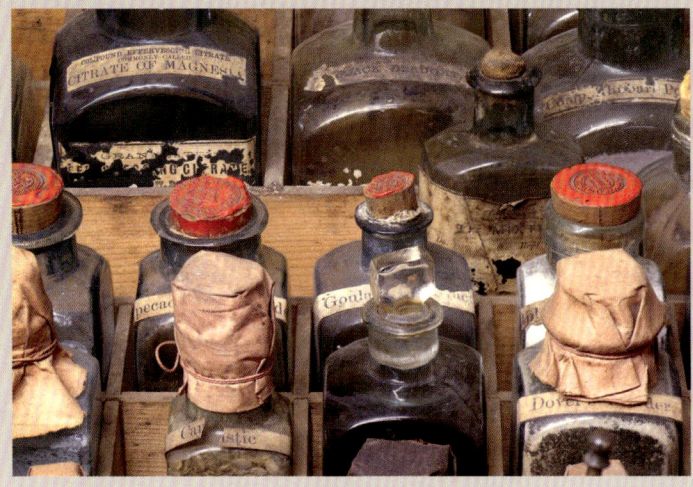

Ship's medicine chest

NETCC: 1985.4851
Given by J.B. Williamson, 1959

The steamship Cormorant was wrecked amidst thick fog on December 21st, 1886, at Whale Chine while carrying a cargo of cotton bales from New Orleans. This ship's medical chest offers a fascinating insight into the ailments of, and treatments available to, sailors at this time. Its contents were all the ship's surgeon would have available to him to treat the various accidents or illnesses which might have befallen the crew while at sea.

The most common ailments seem to have involved digestive issues including constipation and diarrhoea, venereal diseases such as syphilis and various skin conditions such as 'the itch' (scabies). While some of these medicines are still in use in modern times, others have been proven to do as much, if not more, harm than good. Included among the medicines was Tincture of Henbane, used as a narcotic to relieve toothache but also highly poisonous, Tincture of Rhubarb which was one of the safer commonly used drugs and an effective laxative, and 'Blue Pills' which had a range of applications including the treatment of scrofula, jaundice, syphilis and 'cutaneous eruptions' but contained not only calomel and sugar or liquorice to make them palatable but also mercury.

Sponsored by Jonathan Tait

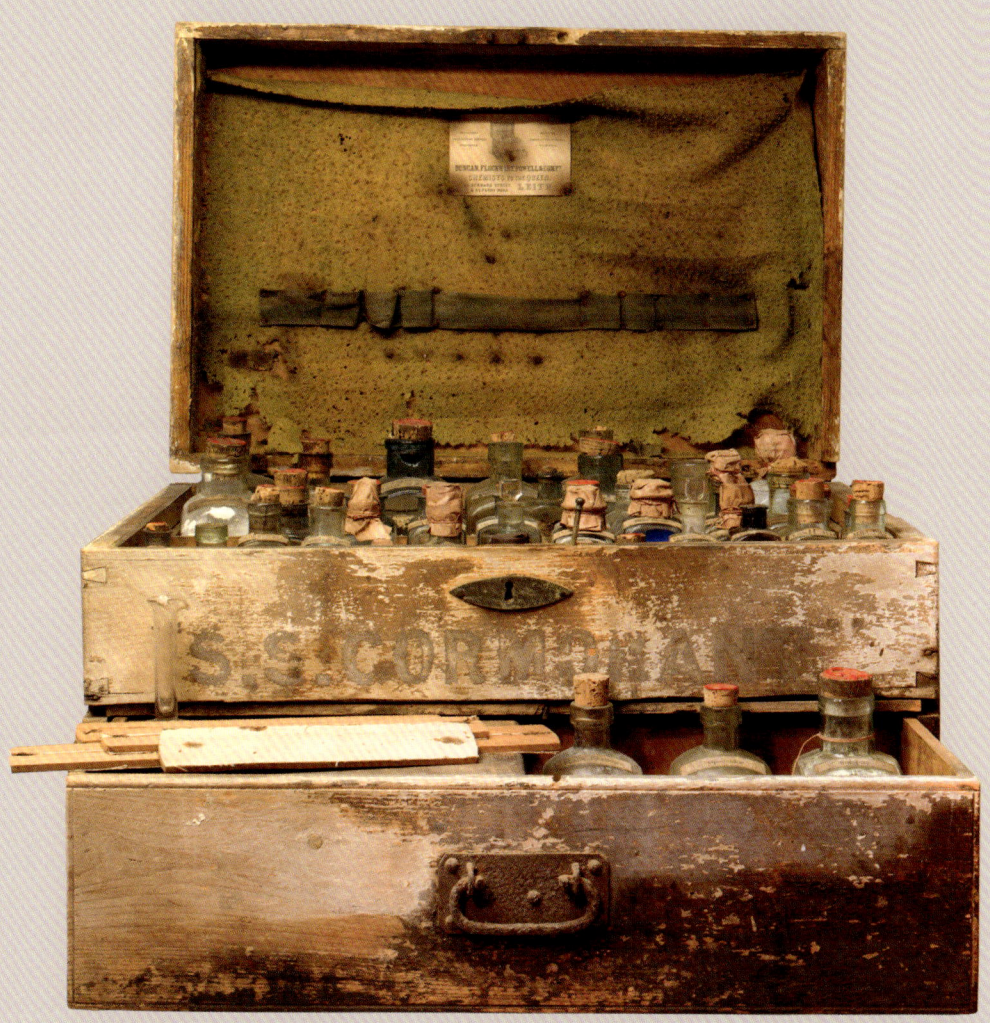

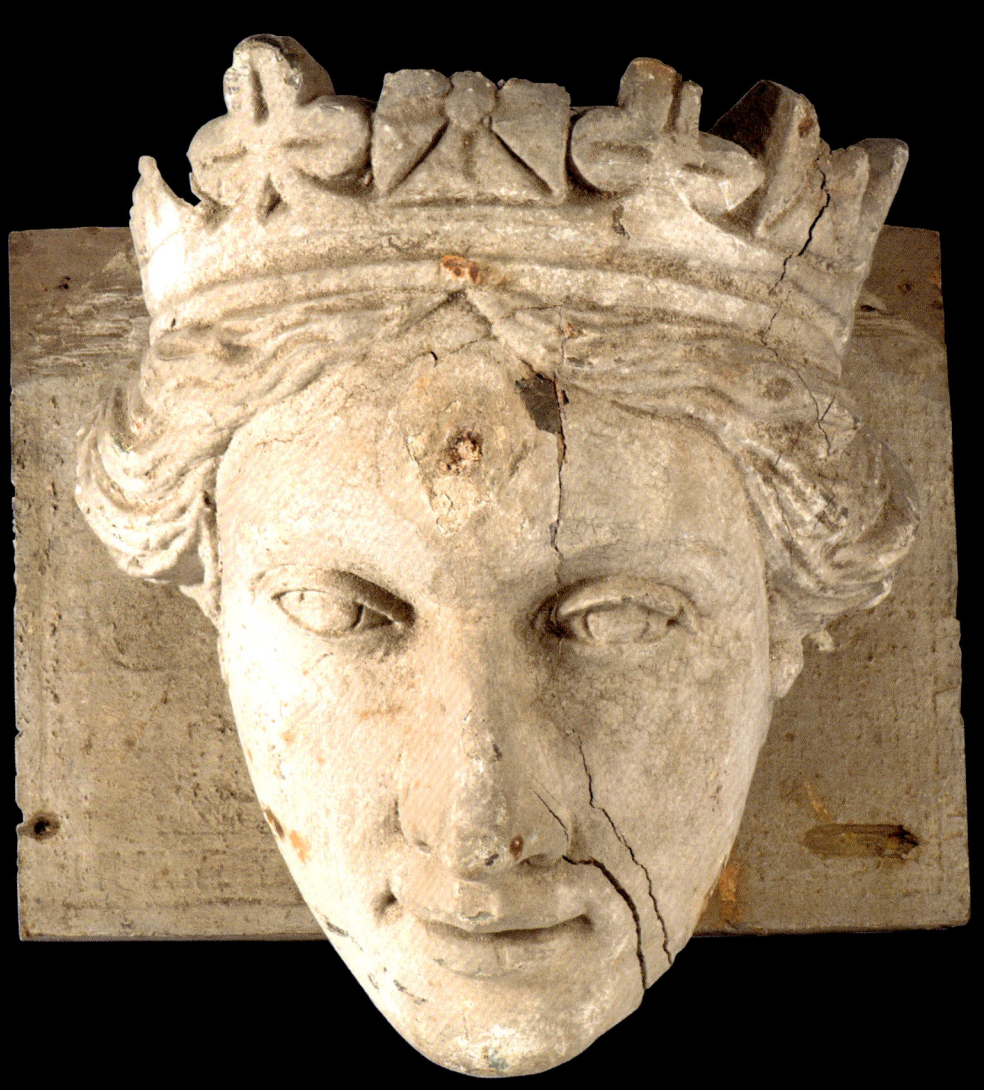

Figurehead of the Auguste of Brake

NETCC: 1985.5252
Lent by G. F. Mew, 1955

Made from carved wood covered in gesso (a type of plaster), this figurehead would have originally been brightly painted. The Auguste of Brake, formerly called Victoria, was wrecked at Atherfield Ledge on February 15th, 1900, during a voyage from Australia to London. A three-masted iron barque, the Auguste was carrying a cargo of jarrah wood, intended to pave streets in London. Several rescue attempts had to be abandoned because of heavy seas and strong winds. The lives of the 18 crew members were finally saved by the Atherfield lifeboat, the Catherine Swift, which brought the men ashore between 3am and 4am. Much of the ship's equipment and cargo were also salvaged before it broke up and was dispersed by the sea.

Sponsored by Diana Parsons

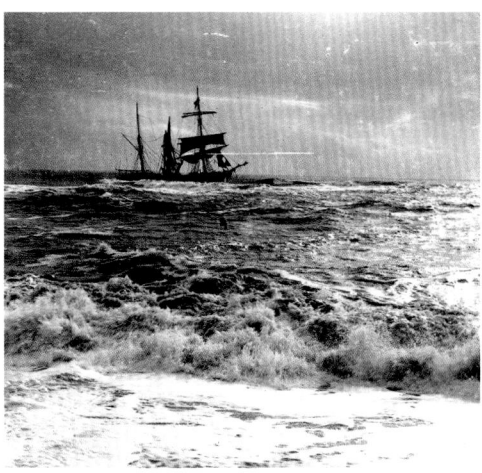

The Auguste of Brake aground on Atherfield Ledge
NETCC: N.1986.939

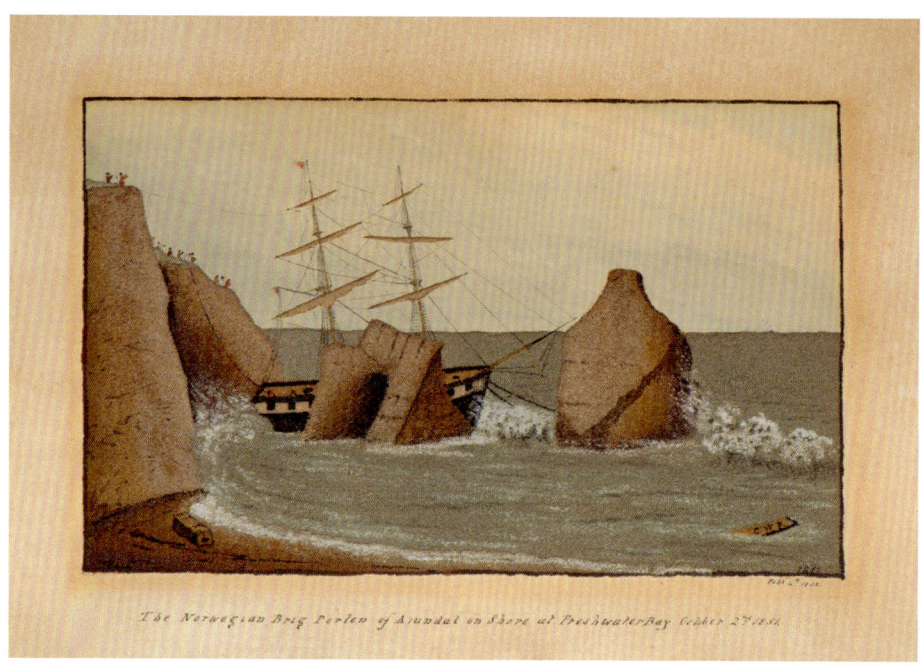

Sand picture of the wrecked Perlen by Charles Plumley

NETCC: P.1986.1544

Given by Miss F.L. Plumley, 1956

Creating and collecting sand pictures and souvenirs was a popular pastime during the Victorian period. The cliffs of Alum Bay supplied the 21 shades of sand used by both professional and amateur artists to make these distinctive Isle of Wight creations.

Charles William Plumley (1823-1896) was a gentleman farmer and an amateur sand artist from Freshwater. Each picture Charles created was probably unique as he was working for his own pleasure rather than the tourist market. This picture of the wreck of the Perlen was executed in February 1852, only a few months after the incident. The Perlen, a Norwegian brig, was on its way from Ireland to Norway when it was driven against the rocks in Freshwater Bay. Charles probably witnessed the wreck and depicted the use of a lifesaving rocket by which all six crew members were safely hauled from the stricken ship to the top of the cliff.

Sponsored for Keith Capelin

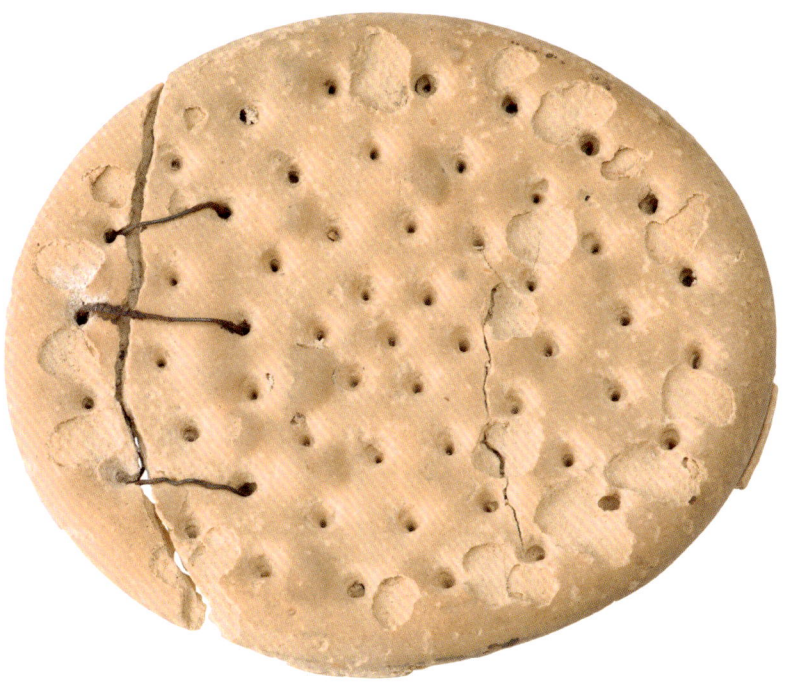

Ship's biscuit from the wreck of the Irex

NETCC: 1985.4818
Given by Lever, 1980

Commonly known as 'hardtack', ship's biscuits were made by baking a dough of flour, water and salt. They were an important part of a sailor's sea diet because they were so long-lasting. The Irex was wrecked at Scratchells Bay in January 1890 whilst on her maiden voyage from Glasgow to Rio de Janeiro with a cargo of iron pipes. Six of the 36 crew members died, while the rest were rescued with a 'Breeches buoy', a winch system similar to a zip line. The trade in souvenirs from wrecks was profitable for locals and many objects and pieces of a ship would often go missing in the aftermath of a wreck. This ship's biscuit was likely a souvenir acquired from the wreck site to sell on.

Sponsored by Sue Bailey of 'But that's another story'

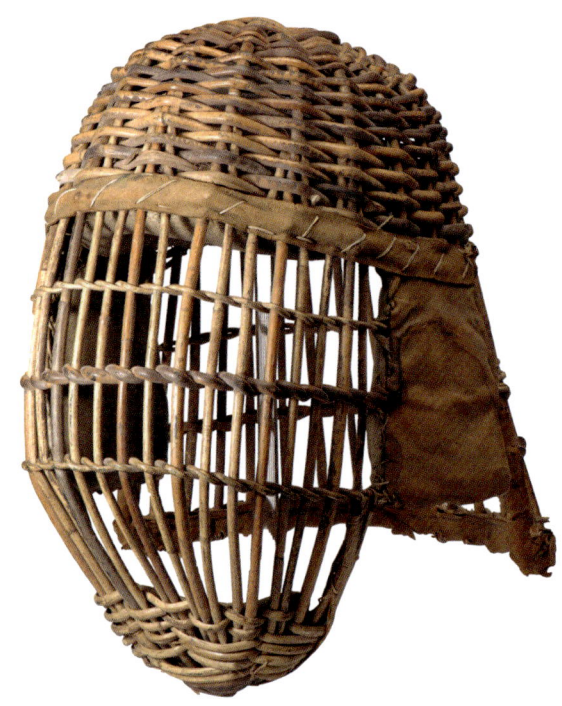

Coastguard helmet

NETCC: 1985.3530
Given by Mr. P. Wootton (H.M. Coastguards, Ventnor), 1960

Coastguards would have used this nineteenth-century basketwork helmet during cliff rescues. Often made by local craftswomen, these helmets protected the wearer not only from small falling rocks, but also from birds they might have disturbed as they traversed the cliff face. When first established, the coastguard's main role was to prevent smuggling. However, they often also became involved in the lifesaving efforts of local lifeboats and, over time, coordinating and supporting the rescue of distressed vessels and people stranded along the coast became as much a part of their role as maritime law enforcement.

Dedicated to Isle of Wight Search & Rescue (WightSAR)

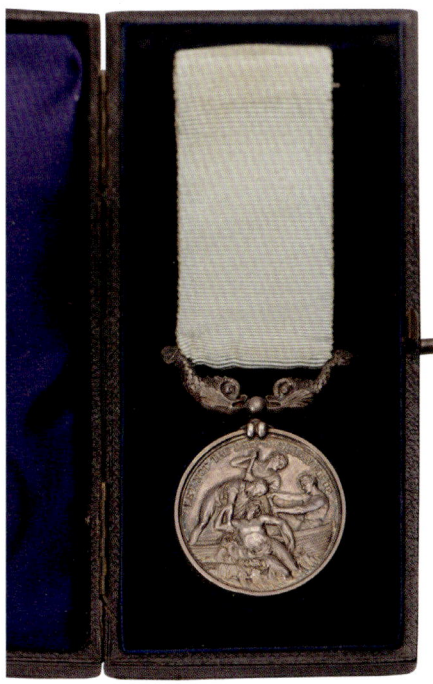

Frank Salter's RNLI medal

NETCC: 1985.1853
Given by M.L. Salter, 1982

This medal was awarded to 19-year-old Frank for his bravery in the rescue of the crew of the Sirenia in March 1888. Sailing with a cargo of wheat from San Francisco and bound for Dunkirk, the Sirenia ran aground in thick fog off Atherfield.

Late in the afternoon, the Brighstone lifeboat launched into heavy seas and rescued the captain's wife and children but then had to wait until low tide. However, by midnight sea conditions worsened so the boat launched again, along with the Brook lifeboat. Disaster struck when the Brighstone boat overturned, throwing its crew and those rescued from the Sirenia into the water while men were also swept from the Brook boat. Three of the lifeboatmen and two of the ship's crew drowned. The next day fresh volunteers launched the Brighstone boat again. Frank was among just three of the original crew fit enough to assist in this final trip out to the stricken ship, bringing the remaining crew back to the beach.

Dedicated to the Isle of Wight RNLI

Carisbrooke Castle by J. M. W. Turner, 1828

By the age of just fifteen Joseph Mallord William Turner (1775-1851) had exhibited his first work at the Royal Academy of Art. Initially establishing a reputation for Romantic watercolour landscapes, the flourishing late eighteenth-century print market provided him with an early commercial opportunity. From the 1790s he made sketching tours around Britain and Europe, and one of his first tours took him to the Isle of Wight in 1795.

This watercolour view of Carisbrooke Castle was painted in 1828 (from a highly finished sketch made during this visit) for the series 'Picturesque Views in England and Wales', a collaborative project between Turner and the printmaker Charles Heath. The series has been described as the 'central document' of Turner's life, and this painting is regarded as one of the finest in the series.

Over time, Turner became a master of oil painting - although the free, expressive, nature of his mature style was shocking to contemporary eyes and received criticism, in the 1840s the influential critic John Ruskin initiated a re-evaluation. Turner is now revered as one of the greatest of all British painters: innovative, technically gifted and a pioneer of Impressionism.

NETCC: 2008.20
Accepted by HM Government in Lieu of Inheritance Tax and allocated to Carisbrooke Castle Museum

Sponsored for Ulrike Schmoranzer

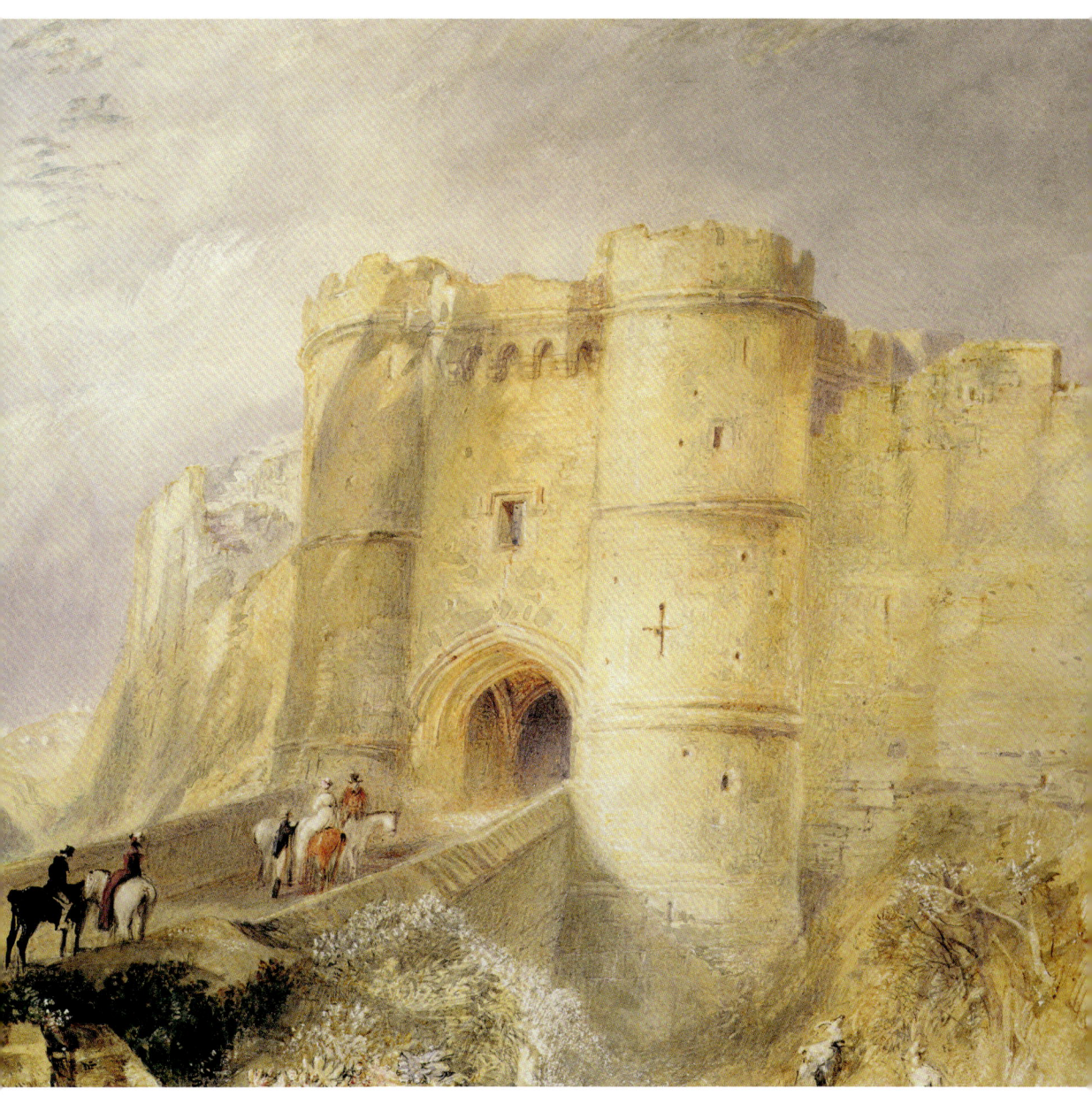

Alfred, Lord Tennyson
'The Dirty Monk' by Julia Margaret Cameron, 1865

NETCC: P.1986.2181

Julia Margaret Cameron (1815-1879) was one of the most important early photographers. Her portraits remain among the most famous of many Victorian celebrities, and her daring experimentation with close-up and diffused focus techniques was pioneering, transforming photography into an art form. She wrote in 1866 that she wanted her work to "electrify you with delight and startle the world."

Julia created almost all her photographs at Dimbola, the house she bought with her husband in Freshwater in the 1860s. An adapted 'glazed fowl house' served as a studio where she photographed local people and servants as well as her famous friends and visitors, including poet Alfred, Lord Tennyson, her neighbour at nearby Farringford. This image, known as the 'Dirty Monk', was radical in its depiction of the renowned poet as wild-haired and brooding and was selected by Alfred as one of his favourite portraits.

Sponsored for Nathan and Maggie Marke

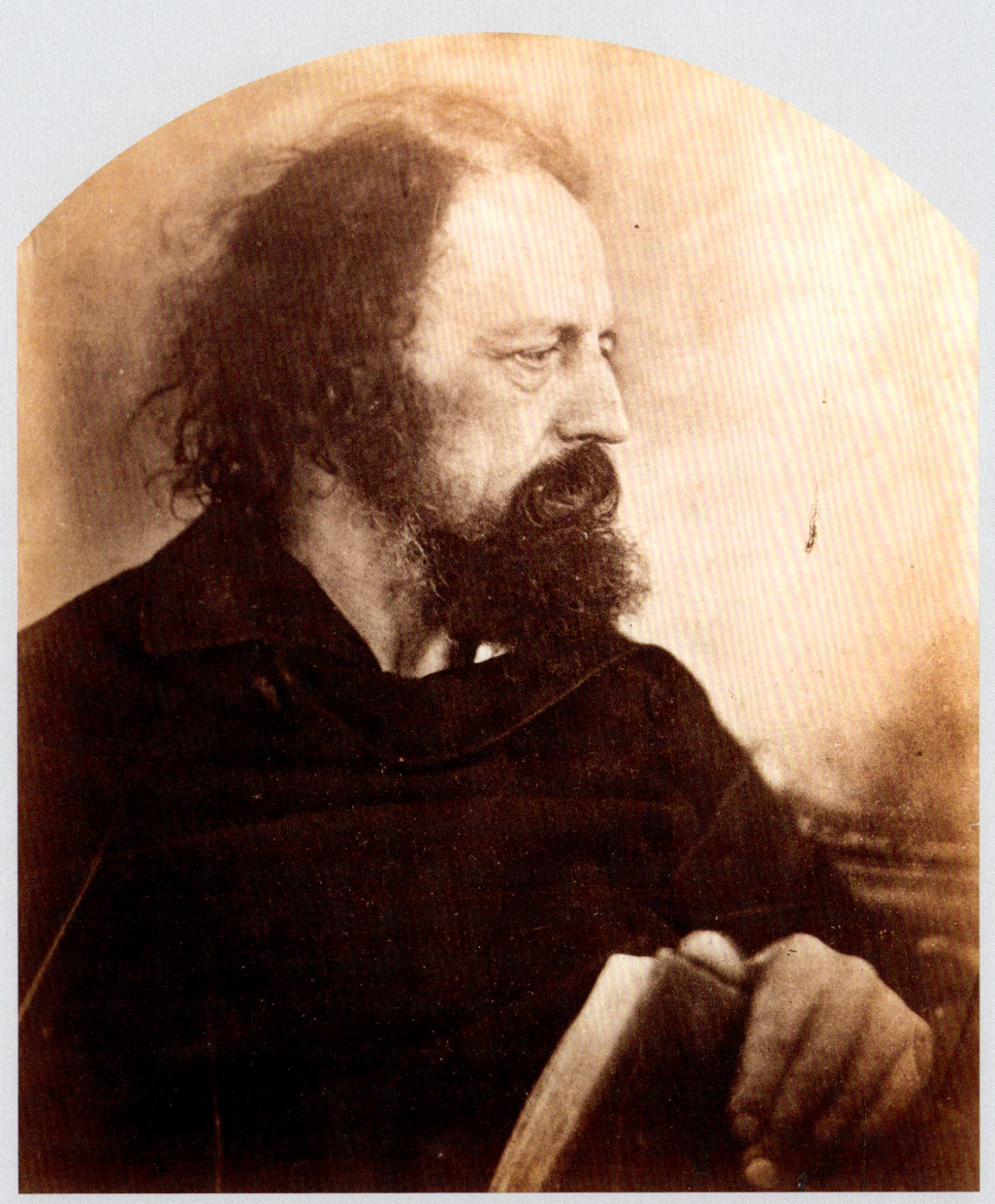

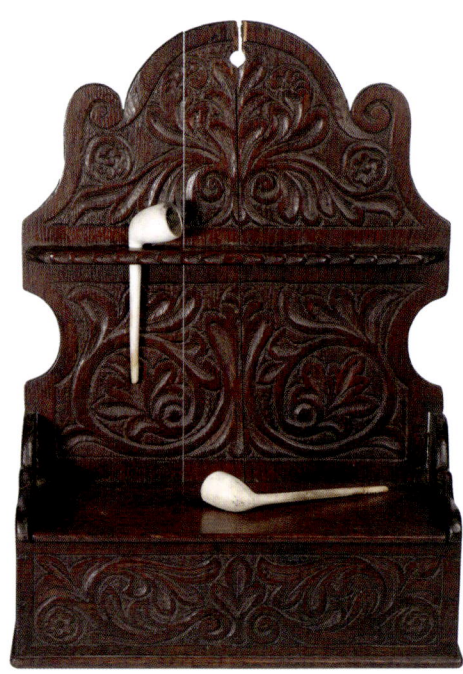

Alfred, Lord Tennyson's pipe rack

NETCC: 1985.5235 L
Lent by David Tennyson

Alfred, Lord Tennyson (1809–1892) was a renowned writer who lived for many years at Farringford in Freshwater. He was Poet Laureate during much of Queen Victoria's reign and remains one of Britain's most popular poets. Admired by both readers and fellow writers, Alfred was ambivalent about his fame and did not enjoy the attention he received from the public. His move to Farringford in 1853 was in part motivated by a desire to escape the demands of London society.

This decision transformed Freshwater into a Victorian tourist attraction. There were many famous visitors at Farringford including Prince Albert and many of the most admired writers, artists and celebrities of the nineteenth century. Along with the photographer Julia Margaret Cameron who lived at nearby Dimbola, Alfred created one of the most renowned creative circles of the age.

Sponsored by David Tennyson

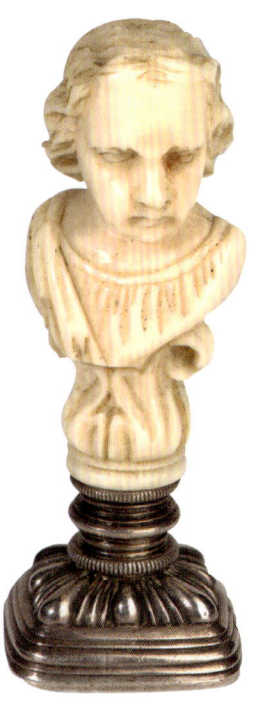

Worsley family seal

NETCC: 1993.265
Purchased, 1993

For three hundred years the Worsleys were the leading family of the Isle of Wight. This seal, probably dating to the Georgian period, features the family crest with three falcons and the family motto: UT SURSUM DE SUPER - Descend to ascend. A carved ivory bust forms the handle and the crest is incised into a bloodstone, coated with silver.

The Worsleys moved to Appuldurcombe in 1690 when the property was inherited by Robert Worsley, 3rd Baronet. Richard Worsley, the 7th Baronet (1751-1805), rebuilt Appuldurcombe in the Palladian style and had the grounds landscaped by Capability Brown. He served as High Sheriff of Hampshire, the MP for Newport and Governor of the Isle of Wight.

Sponsored by Seaview Art Gallery

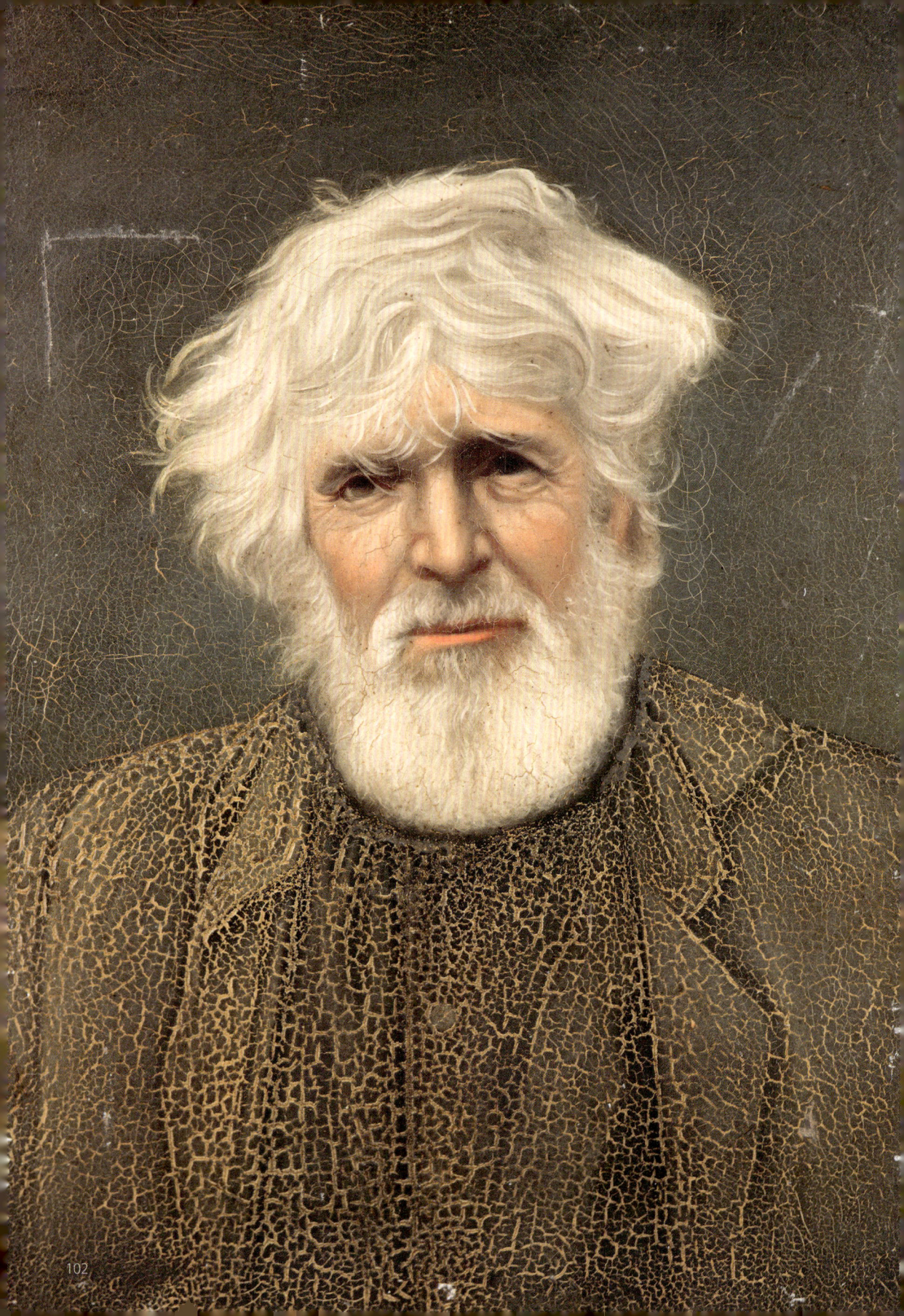

Charles 'Pound Hammer' Kingswell

NETCC: 1995.497
Given by C. Holbrook, 1995

Charles, who was born in about 1810, lived with his wife Jane, who was born in Jamaica in a small cottage at Luccombe Chine. They were part of a small fishing community that lived practically on the shore in the nineteenth century. He was widely known by his nickname 'Pound Hammer' although the origins of this name are uncertain. Their cottage was small but had a long garden in which a chapel was built for the use of local families. However, a difference of opinion arose between Pound Hammer and his neighbours and he refused to allow any of them into his garden, so ultimately the chapel was not used and another was built further along the shore. According to local legend, the now unused chapel was eventually taken down to the beach and floated along the shore to Shanklin and re-erected there. The cottages have now all been lost due to landslips and coastal erosion.

Sponsored by Kirsti Cousins

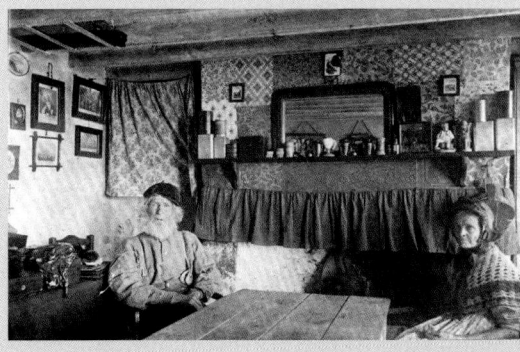

Charles and Mary Kingswell in their cottage at Luccombe Chine
NETCC: 2010.135

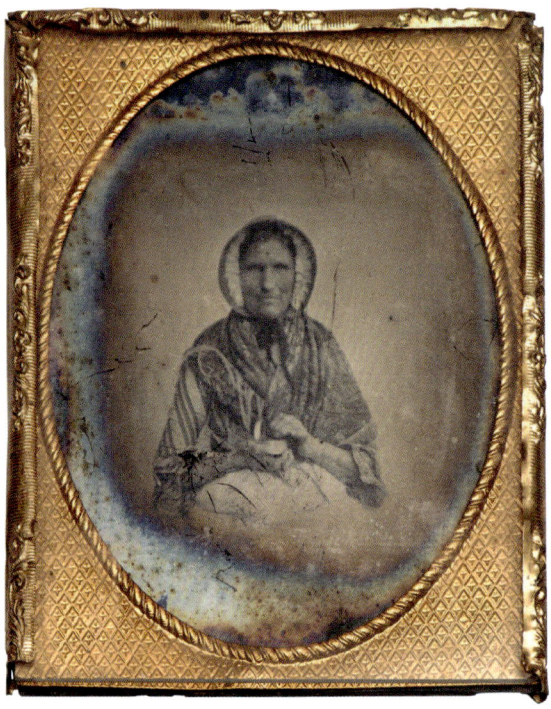

Ambrotype of Mary Merwood

NETCC: P.1986.1984

Mary Merwood (1786-1877) lived at One Tree Cottage on St Georges Down for many years with her husband John. She spun wool and made the heads of mops while John made the wooden handles. She also sold refreshments to travellers passing by on the way from Arreton to Shide, using water from what became known as Mary Merwood's well. When John died in 1869, Mary moved to Kingston, near Shorwell, to live with the Cheek family. She died in 1877 and is buried at Arreton.

Taken in 1858, this ambrotype is a type of early photograph in which a unique image is created on a glass plate. Because the technique only produced one image, it was soon superseded by methods that could be used to create multiple prints.

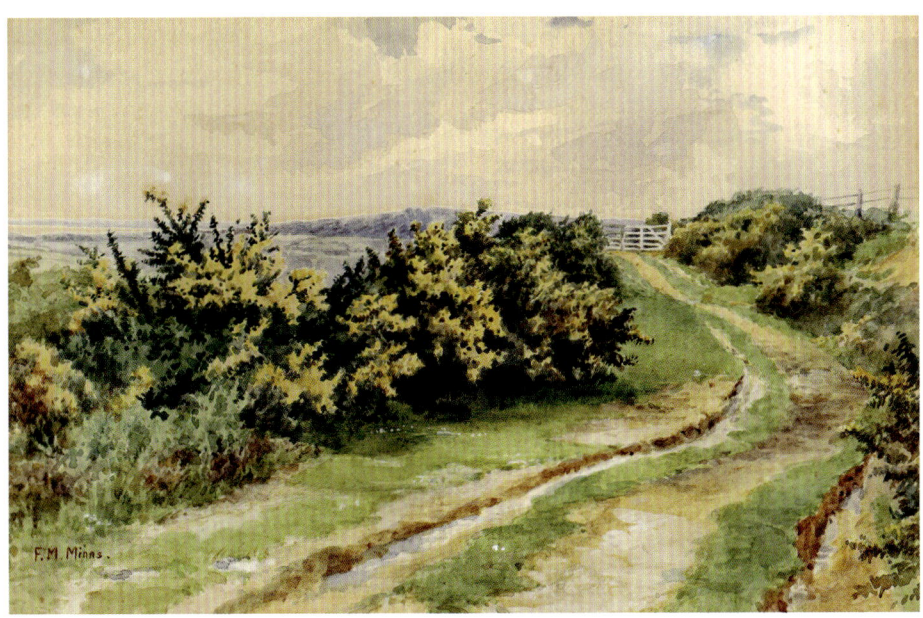

Watercolour of Pan Down by Fanny Minns

NETCC: P.1986.1371
Given by Lady K.M. Maybury, 1970

Fanny (1847-1929) was the daughter of William Minns and Mary Bright of Bright and Minns Ltd, dyers and dry cleaners of Nodehill, Newport, from 1833-1997. The family's business success allowed her the luxury of training as an artist. She likely received painting lessons from another local woman artist Ellen Cantelo and then, because women were not admitted to the Royal Academy in London, she trained at the Dresden Art Academy.

Working in watercolour she produced landscapes of local views, working outside or 'en plein air' to capture the immediacy of light and colour. Her travels took her to Switzerland and she exhibited widely in Britain, including at the Birmingham Art Gallery, the Walker Gallery in Liverpool, and the Royal Society of British Artists. She also produced postcards and was commissioned to illustrate several books including the work of fellow-Islander Maxwell Grey.

Sponsored by Nick and Val Minns

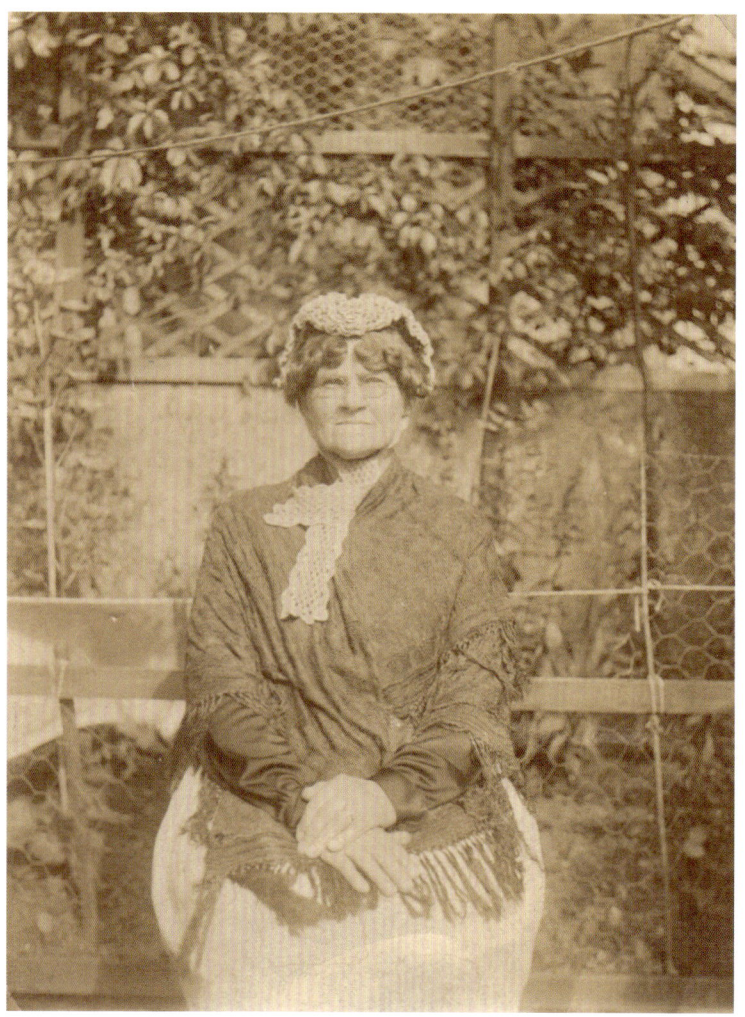

Mrs Saunders
NETCC: 2001.7

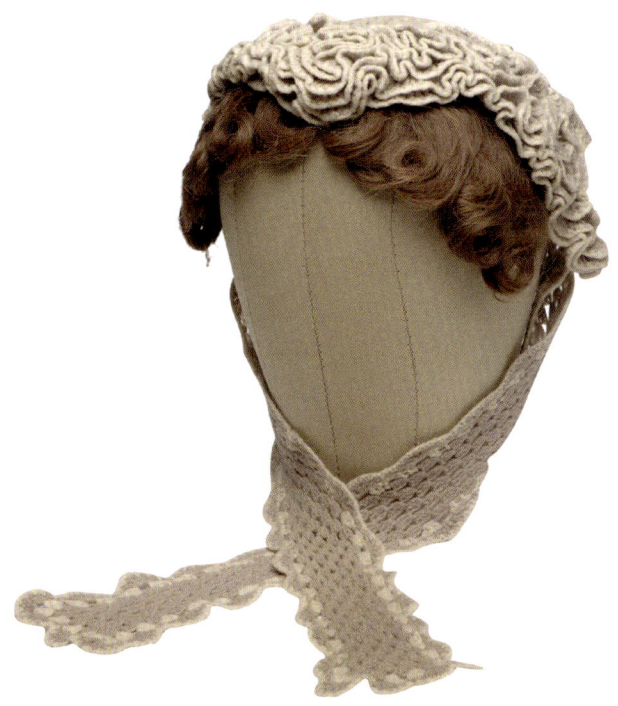

Hairpiece and crocheted bonnet

NETCC: 2001.5-6
Given by Mrs Auchterlonie, 2001

This hairpiece is made of real human hair and was worn by a lady who lived in Newport. It is unusual not only for the wig and bonnet but also for a photograph of their owner wearing them to have survived together. Her surname was possibly Saunders and she died in about 1890. The fashion at this time was for long hair to be dressed in curls and if your own hair couldn't be styled this way you could use a hairpiece to achieve the effect. Hair merchants imported human hair from Europe to make wigs and hairpieces. Poor and desperate women might turn to the sale of their hair as a means of survival.

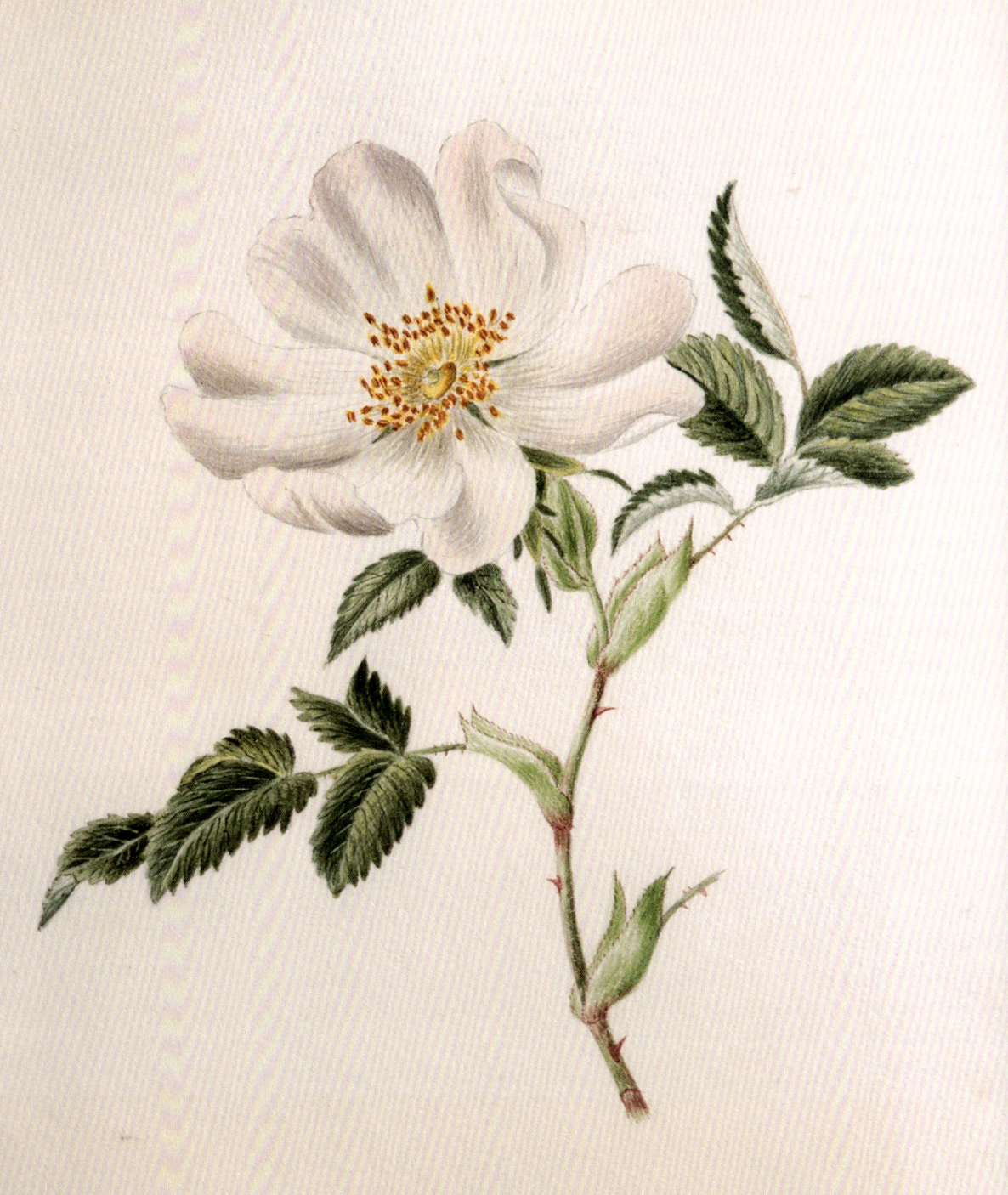

Emma Denett's botanical album

NETCC: 2017.5
Given by Jane Erith, 2016

This album, which was created between 1846 and 1847, is a valuable record of the flora of the Isle of Wight in the nineteenth century. Emma's watercolours record the wildflowers and plants growing near her home; the delicate images are accompanied by both the Latin and common names of the plants, along with the date and location in which she found them. Botanical painting was a common hobby of Victorian ladies, but this album is of interest to modern-day botanists. Many species no longer occur in the localities where Emma found them while others have been newly discovered in recent years, still growing in the places she recorded them. Emma was the daughter of John Dennett, a custodian of Carisbrooke Castle and inventor of a lifesaving rocket. Emma was born in 1814 and was brought up in New Village and Carisbrooke and lived mostly with her brothers and sisters after their parents died.

Sponsored in loving memory of Laraine Pascoe

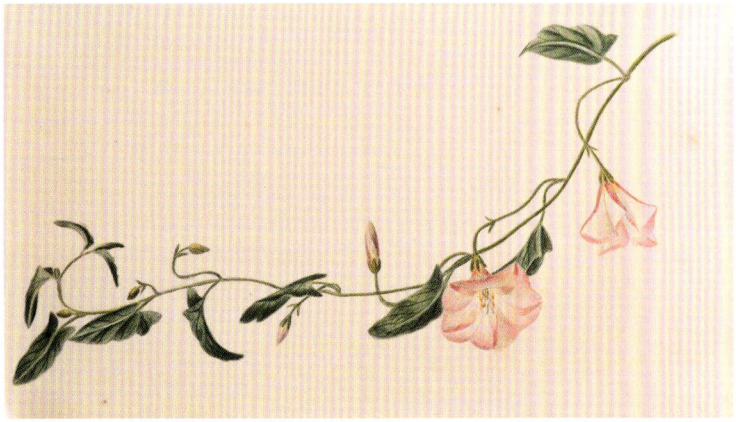

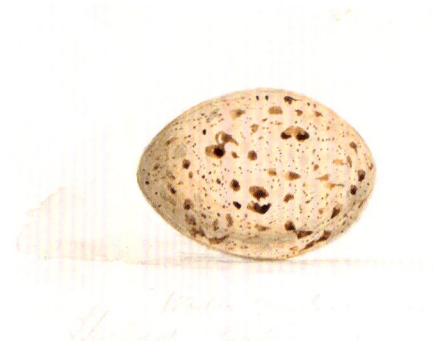
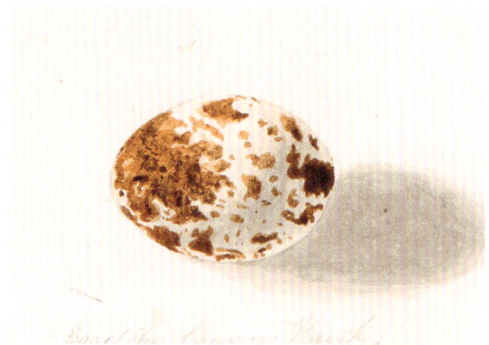

Study of bird eggs by Harriet Darwin Fox, 1839

NETCC: D.1986.1076
Given by H. F. Poole, 1957

These eggs, of a Spotted Gallinule (now more commonly known as a Spotted Crake) and a Sparrow Hawk, were painted by Harriet Darwin Fox. The Spotted Gallinule, a small wading bird, has always been a rare breeding bird in this country and the nests are notoriously difficult to find. The eggs were collected by Harriet's husband, the Rev. William Darwin Fox (1805-1880), who was a clergyman, naturalist and an entomologist. William had prepared for the Church at Cambridge alongside his younger cousin Charles Darwin whom he tutored in natural history. He took up a curacy near Nottingham but after an illness came to Sandown to convalesce in 1833. When he retired in 1873, he returned to the Island and lived the rest of his life at Broadlands, Sandown. These studies are believed to be the sole surviving remnants of a collection created by the Darwin Foxes for Charles Darwin.

Sponsored by John and Tina Lucas

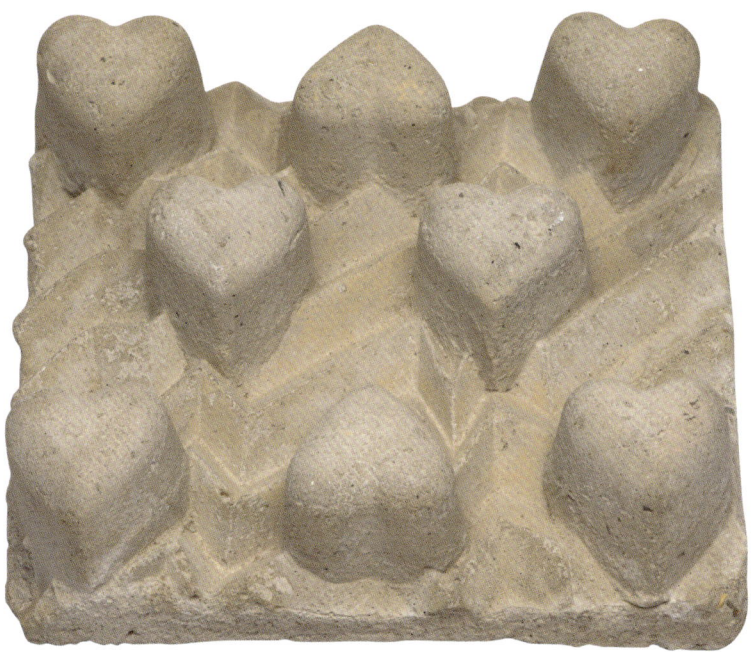

Eel pass tile

NETCC: 2022.102 (L)
Lent by Artecology

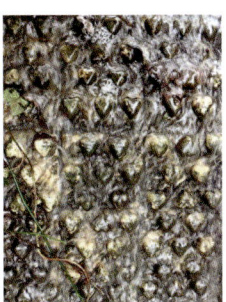

Eel pass tiles in-situ at Holbrookes Stream (© Artecology)

First developed for a culvert on Holbrookes Stream in Yarmouth, this 'heart and dart' style tile is cast in reduced-carbon concrete and was designed to aid the migration of European eels (Anguilla anguilla) up river and past man-made obstacles. The tile provides flow control and texture purchase for the eels to move upstream and the large area created by the folded surface also provides a range of micro-sites to support wildlife.

It was created in 2017 by Artecology, the research and development department of Arc Biodiversity & Climate based in Sandown. Their mixed-discipline design team works on bringing new eco-engineering ideas to life, helping to bring wildlife to urban spaces and places.

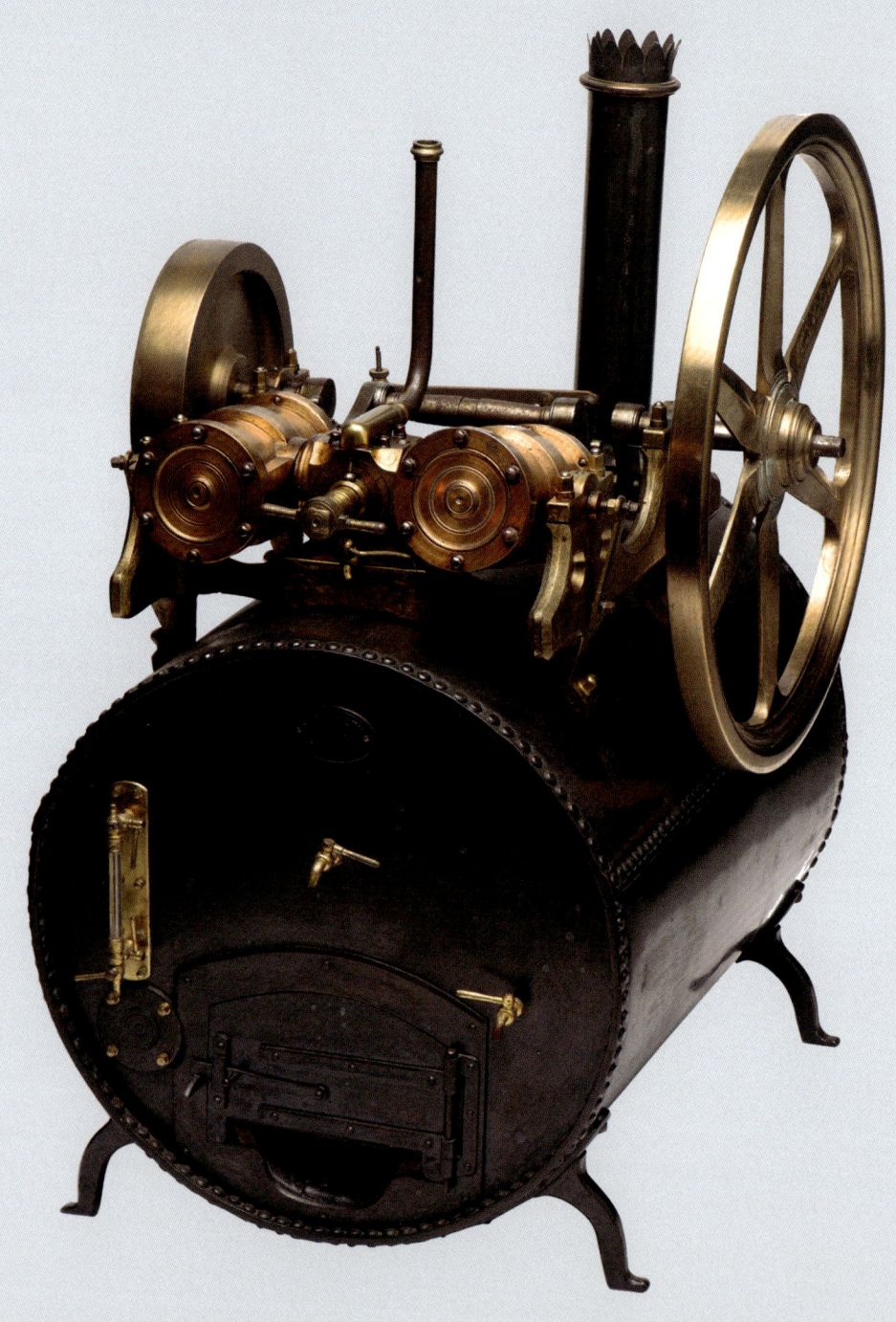

Horatio Dennett's model steam engine

NETCC: 1985.5446
Given by F.E. Hunter, 1976

In a local directory of 1859, Horatio was listed as a 'rocket manufacturer'. The rocket, developed by his father John, could fire a line over to a ship in distress, and after his father's death, Horatio took over the family business. On the Island, three rocket stations were established at Freshwater, Atherfield and St Lawrence. These stations successfully deployed the device to rescue survivors from various wrecks, saving 19 individuals from the Bainbridge in 1832 and 36 from the Irex in 1890.

Horatio inherited his father's engineering skills and creativity and undertook various jobs, in 1875 referring to himself as 'a civil engineer' and in 1878 a 'brick manufacturer'. He made this working model of a steam engine in 1846.

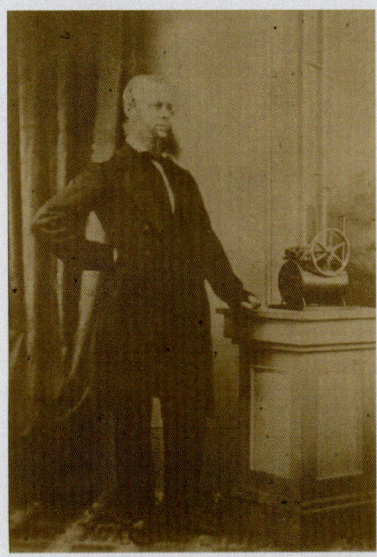

Horatio Dennett with his model steam engine
NETCC: 2016.458

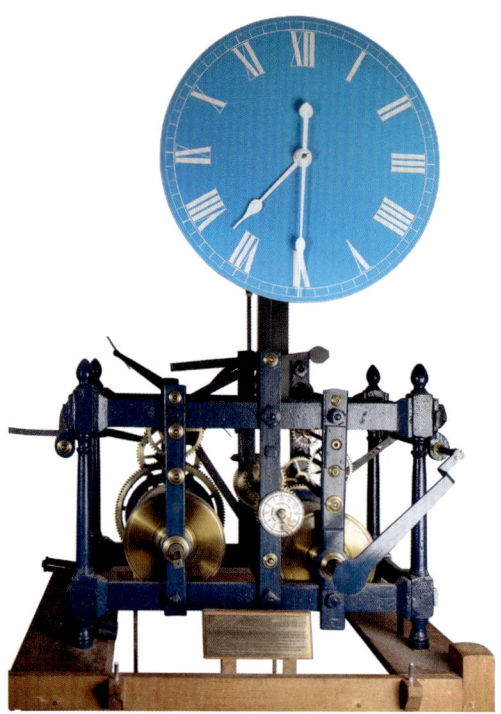

Clock from East Cowes Castle

NETCC: 1995.282
Given by the Isle of Wight College, 1995

This clock was originally installed on the turret of East Cowes Castle, a Gothic-style mansion designed by architect John Nash, one of the most famous architects of the eighteenth and early nineteenth centuries. Responsible for much of the layout of Regency London, his work included the Royal Pavilion, Brighton, and Buckingham Palace. Nash first visited the Isle of Wight in 1793 and in 1798 bought the estate where he would construct East Cowes Castle. He designed or altered many buildings on the Island, including Newport Guildhall.

Made in 1819 by John Moore of Clerkenwell, London, the clock was the first of eleven made for Island buildings, including the town halls in Newport and Ryde. After East Cowes Castle was demolished in 1960, the clock movement was rescued by local councillor Arthur Guy who presented it to the Isle of Wight College where it was restored under the guidance of Ifan Thorner and John French.

Sponsored by Graham Petrie

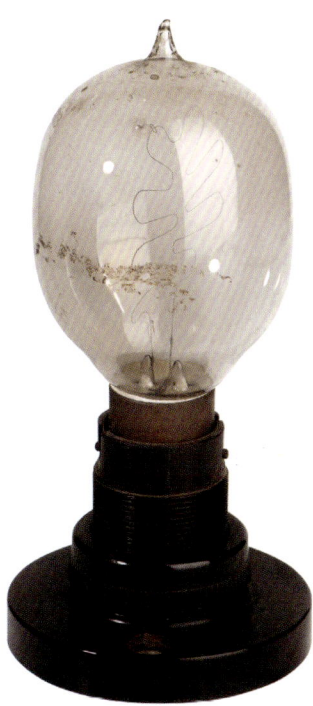

'Sunbeam' lightbulb

NETCC: 1985.2474
Given by Dr. J. B. Williamson, 1955

This incandescent lightbulb, produced by Sunbeam and featuring a Bakelite bayonet fitting, was one of the first ever installed in Ventnor. In 1899 the town gained the Island's first public electric supply, provided by the Ventnor Electric Light and Power Company Ltd. The company, a partnership between the Edmundsons Electrical Corporation who operated in the South of England and Ventnor Town Council, had a generating station on Mitchell Avenue near the town's train station (and a ready supply of coal). While previously most urban areas of the Island had a town gas supply to light streets and buildings, within a year of opening the company was renamed the Isle of Wight Electric Light and Power Company Ltd as they rapidly expanded across the Island.

Sponsored for OnTheWight

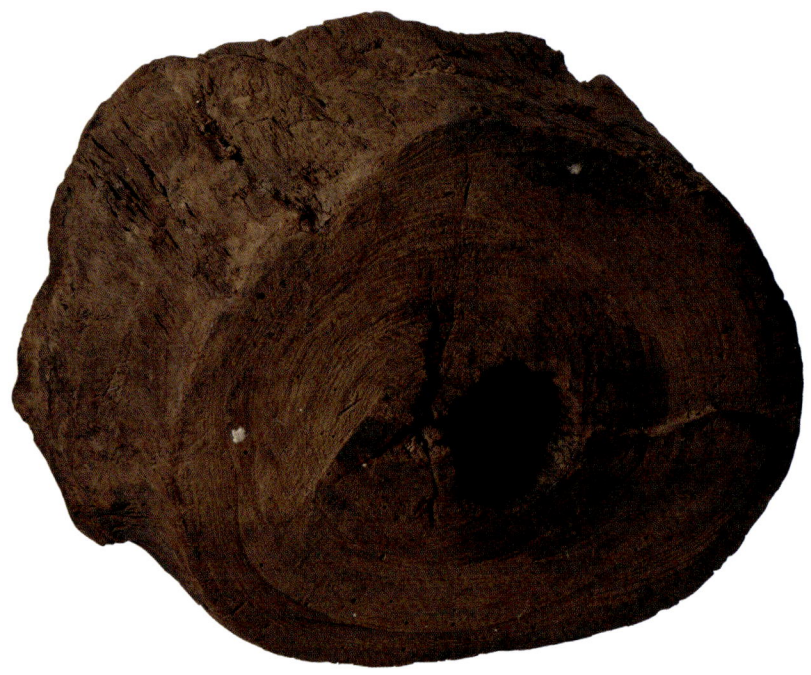

Wooden water mains pipe

NETCC: 1985.4737

This wooden pipe was laid in the seventeenth century to carry a mains water supply to houses in Newport High Street. In 1618 and again in 1623 pipes made of bored-out elm trunks were installed beneath the street, with the sections of trunk tapered at one end to join to the next section of pipe. However, the system never worked and it was not until the nineteenth century that the town had a serviceable mains water system. Until a working system was installed, households without their own wells could buy water from a water cart. Several pieces of pipe have been discovered in excavations. This piece was unearthed when a gas pipe was being laid in the 20th century.

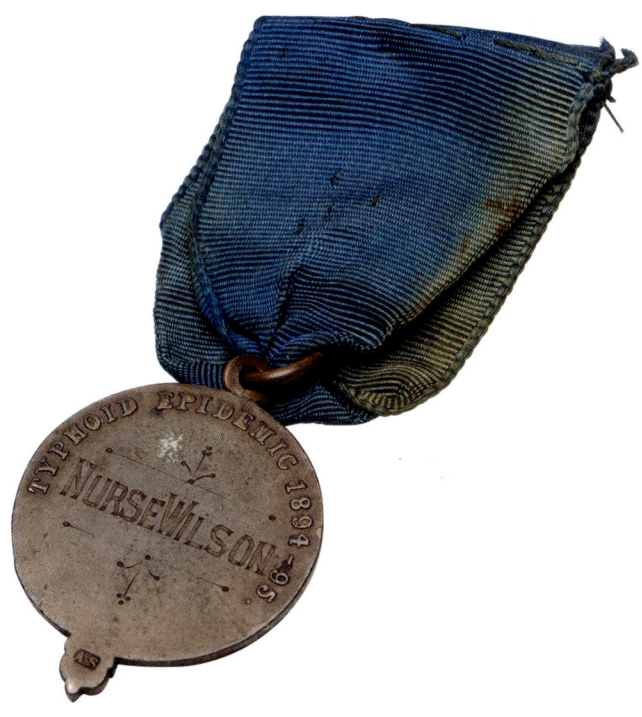

Nurse Wilson's typhoid epidemic medal

NETCC: 1985.1845

This bronze medal was one of nine awarded to nurses on the Isle of Wight after the Newport Typhoid epidemic of 1894-5. The outbreak was blamed on the contamination of the town's water supply, which was not surprising given that raw sewage was deposited into the Lukely stream and the River Medina which both flow into Newport Quay. It was reported that "on a hot summer day the sewage stewed in the sun on an ebbing tide" and there were also concerns voiced about the high number of open pigsties in the town. Typhoid, known as 'bowel fever' was a serious and potentially deadly illness; the first effective vaccine was introduced in 1896.

Dedicated to the doctors, nurses and care staff with thanks for all they did throughout the Covid pandemic

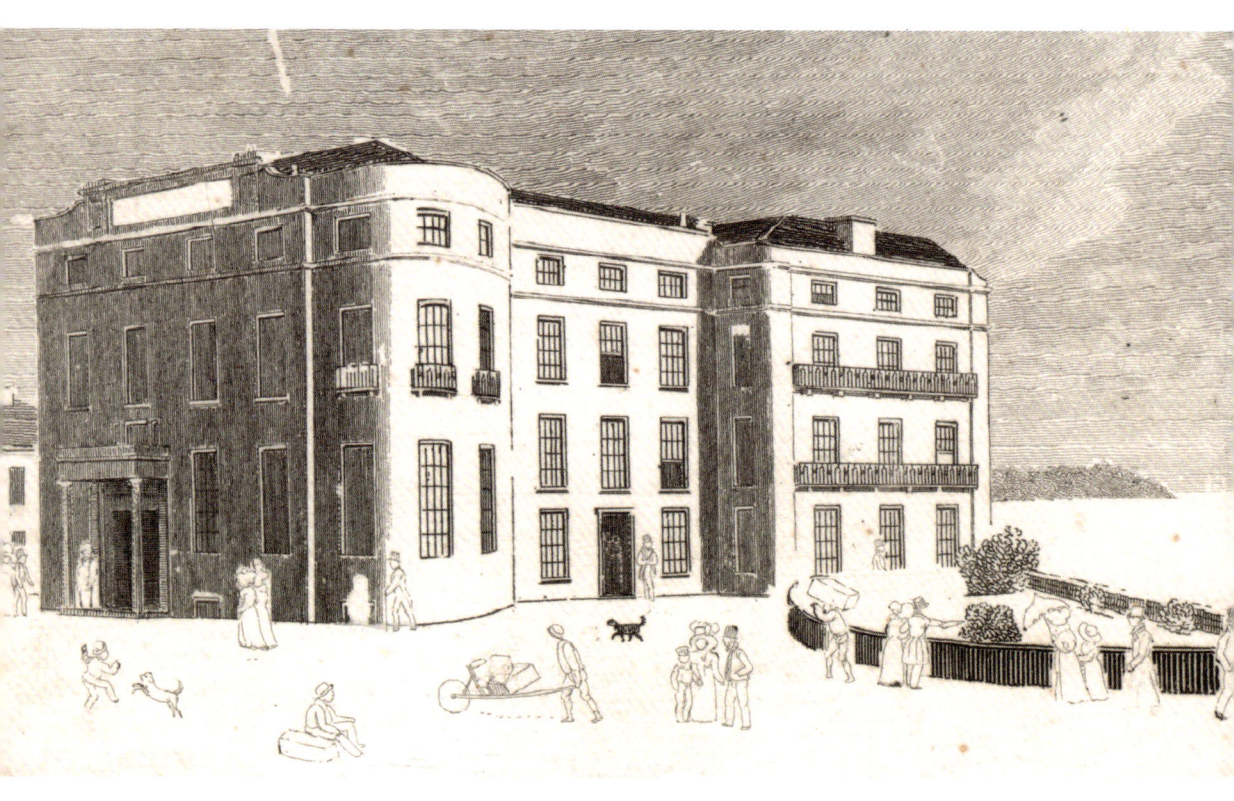

George Brannon artist's proof

NETCC: 2018.312
Given by the Isle of Wight County Press, 2017

This print is an artist-proof created by George Brannon (1784-1860), a prolific artist and engraver who produced hundreds of views of the Island in the early nineteenth century, including his best-known work the book, 'Vectis Scenery', which was first published in 1821. Engraving is an 'intaglio' printing method in which an image is created, in reverse, on the printing plate with various sharp tools. Ink is rubbed onto the plate then its surface is wiped clean, leaving the ink in the incised indentations. The ink is transferred, creating the printed image, when the plate and a sheet of damp paper are passed through a printing press.

Engravers created test prints as they worked and in this image of the Pier Hotel in Ryde, you can see George has begun to outline the building and figures but is still at an early stage of the process with much detail to add. The museum holds a large collection of plates and prints that were passed down through the Brannon family and then held by the Isle of Wight County Press, founded by George's grandson, also called George, in 1884. This includes a number of other proofs which have been annotated and drawn into by hand.

Sponsored by Steve Porter

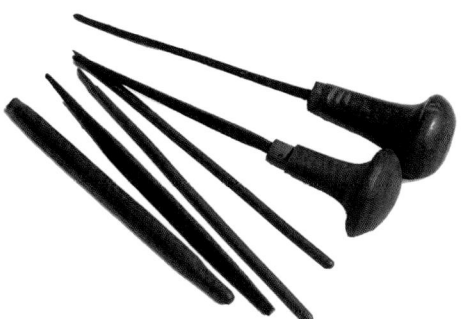

Brannon's engraving tools
NETCC: 2018.240

Professor John Milne's laboratory at Shide Hill House

John Milne (1850-1913) was a founder of the science of seismology, the study of earthquakes. Born in Liverpool, he trained at King's College London and the Royal School of Mines and was appointed Professor of Geology and Mining at the newly formed Imperial College of Engineering, Tokyo. Following the devastating Yokohama earthquake of 1880, he took a special interest in earthquakes and helped found the Seismological Society of Japan.

John's pioneering work included the development of the first seismograph capable of recording major earthquakes occurring in any part of the world. In 1895, he and his wife Toné moved to Shide Hill House near Newport where he established the world's first seismographic station.

This photograph features the couple with the prominent Russian physicist, Prince Boris Galitzin in the laboratory at Shide with John's remarkable 'lamp post' seismograph – essentially a horizontal pendulum seismograph built on a huge scale, using as the vertical support a commercial cast iron lamp post supplied by Hursts of Newport.

This photograph may have been taken by John's assistant Shinobu Hirota. When a second seismograph was installed at Carisbrooke Castle, Shinobu faithfully walked four miles daily, regardless of the weather, to maintain it. A working seismograph can be seen at the museum today.

NETCC: N.1986.913

Sponsored for Vix Lowthion

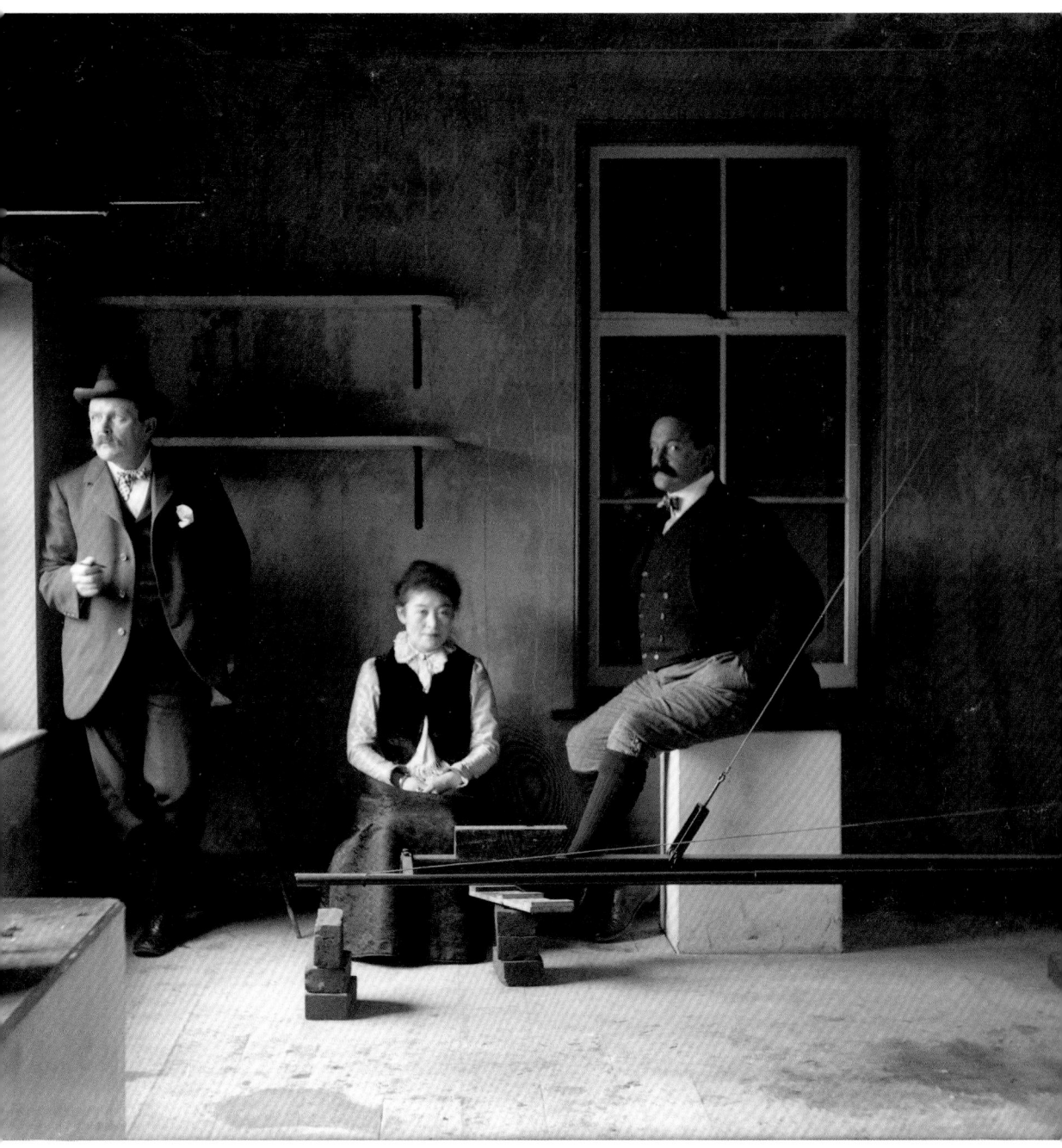

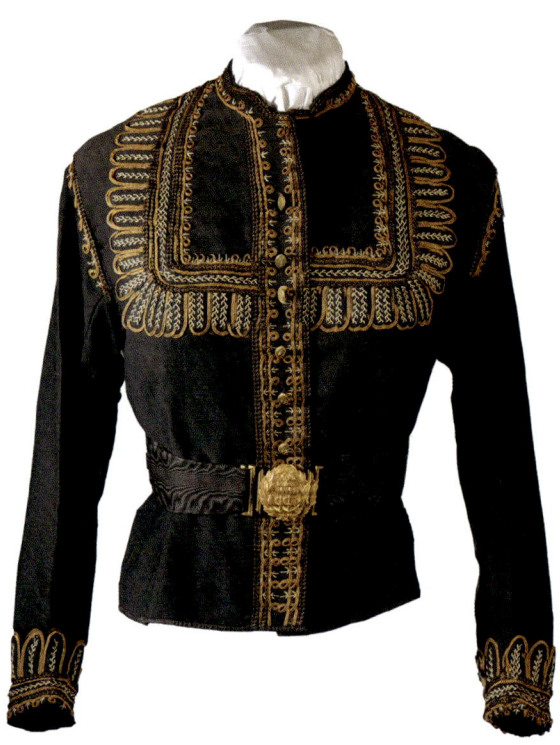

Yachting bodice

NETCC: 1985.3376
Given by Rachel Hotham, 1983

During the late nineteenth century, Cowes was home to Admiral Sir Algernon de Horsey, his wife Caroline Augusta, and their four children (Louisa, Spencer, Muriel, and Grace). This yachting bodice most likely belonged to Grace de Horsey and would have been worn on board the Admiral's yacht, Wych. During Cowes Week the town transformed into a glittering social spectacle and the fashionable world filled every hotel and house. Wych competed in several races during the Cowes regatta but was also used by the Admiral and his daughters. This bodice was worn as part of an outfit with a matching skirt, silk gloves and a straw boater hat.

Sponsored by Shirley Hill

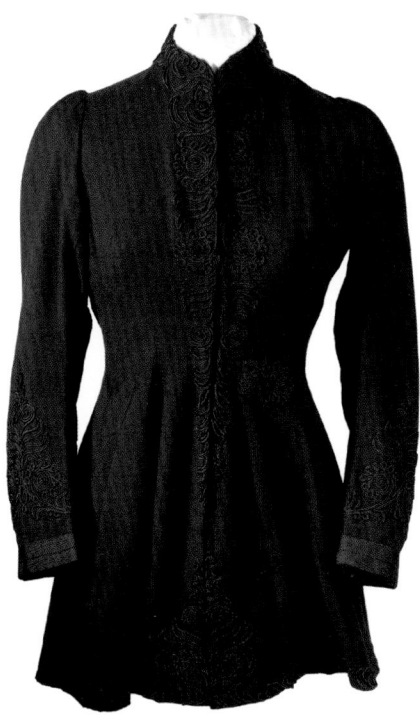

Redfern and Sons 'tailor-made' style jacket

NETCC: 1985.3328

In the 1840s, John Redfern established a linen drapery business at 41 High Street, Cowes. The shop benefited from its proximity to Osborne House and the Cowes Regatta, attracting royal and wealthy customers. Redfern's started making yachting outfits and practical 'tailor-made' ensembles in the 1870s. These were popularised by fashionable women of the day and over the next 20 years Redfern's opened branches in London, Paris and New York, transforming a small drapery business into an international fashion enterprise.

This braided black wool jacket, dating to the 1880s or 90s, would have been worn as part of a 'tailor-made' ensemble; an outfit made using the cutting and fitting principles and fabrics of men's suits. As more women participated in sports and entered the workplace, there were significant changes in women's fashion and 'tailor-made' outfits became acceptable daywear and the forerunner to modern women's suits.

Sponsored by Montgomery Estate Planning Limited

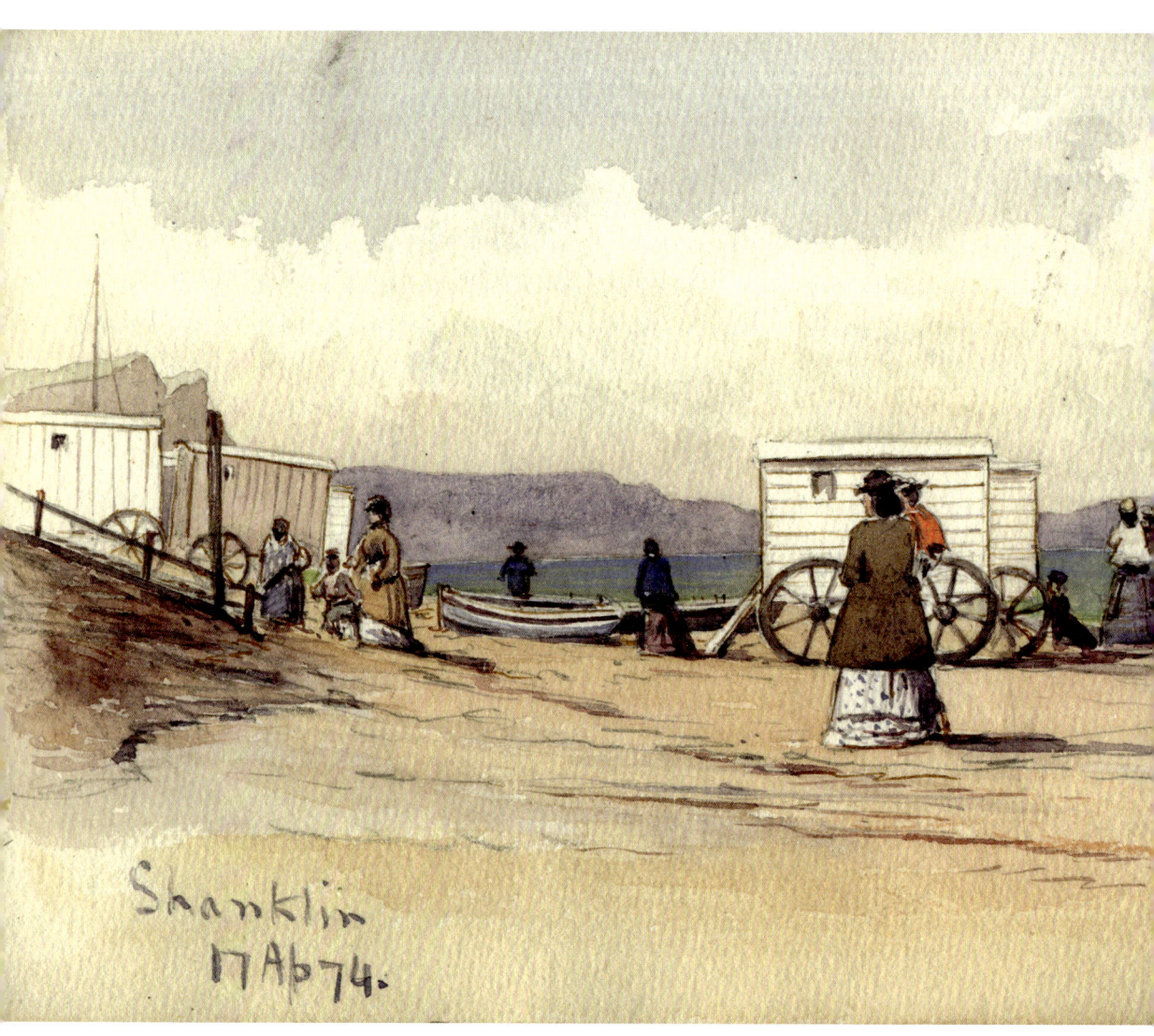

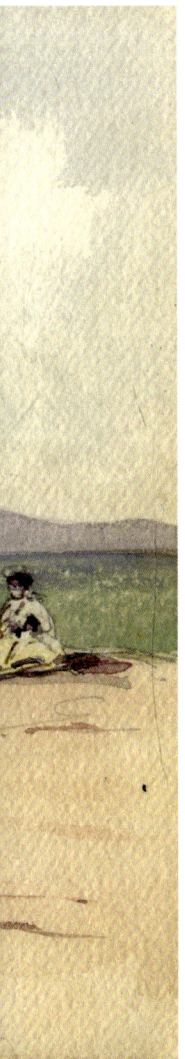

Shanklin beach by Alfred Harcourt, 1874

The growing popularity of the seaside holiday and saltwater bathing in the nineteenth century transformed Shanklin from a quiet village to a busy tourist resort. The growing railway network on the Isle of Wight and the presence of Queen Victoria at Osborne House also encouraged visitors to come to the Island. Shanklin became popular for its mineral baths with mineral-rich spring waters piped to the Royal Spa Hotel. Sea bathing was also considered to be healthy and bathing machines soon became a familiar sight on beaches throughout Europe. While a number of bathing machines can be seen in this watercolour, the coats worn by the beachgoers suggest that it may have been too cold to go swimming! This charming painting is from a sketchbook in which the artist recorded the people and places he observed whilst staying at Culver House in Shanklin.

NETCC: 2013.1.12
Given by Patton, Sonja and Maya Eidson, 2012

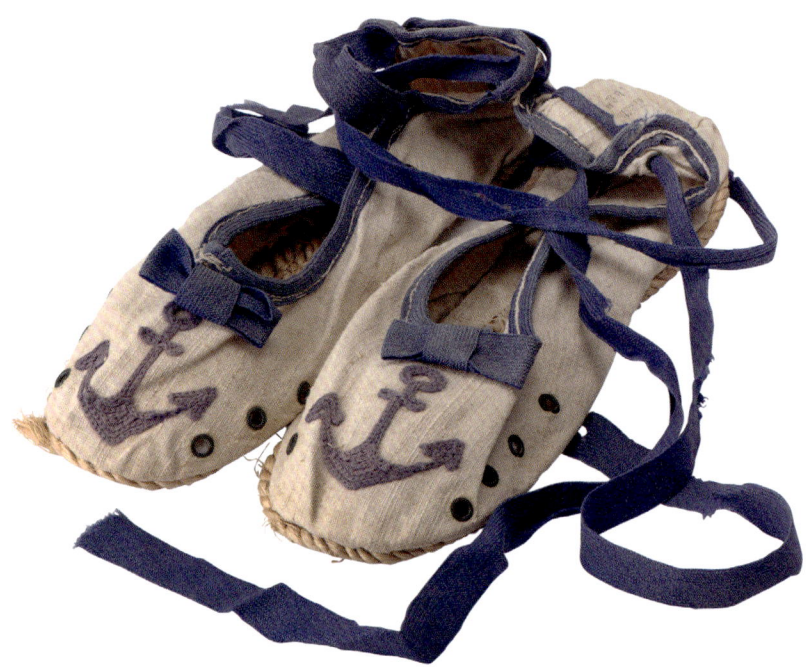

Empress Eugénie's bathing shoes

NETCC: 1985.3621
Given by Hollis

Also known as sand shoes or bathing slippers, canvas and rope-soled shoes quickly became popular beach wear for women and would have been tied with ribbons wound around the ankles or up the leg. They provided much-needed protection for the feet from stony beaches, sharp shells and broken glass. Often damaged beyond repair by seawater, these rare survivors were probably made in France.

They belonged to Empress Eugénie (1826-1920) who, after the overthrow of the French Second Empire with France's defeat in the Franco-Prussian War, took permanent refuge in England with her husband Napoleon III and their son. She was great friends with Queen Victoria and Princess Beatrice and would visit them at Osborne House.

Sponsored by Patricia Franks

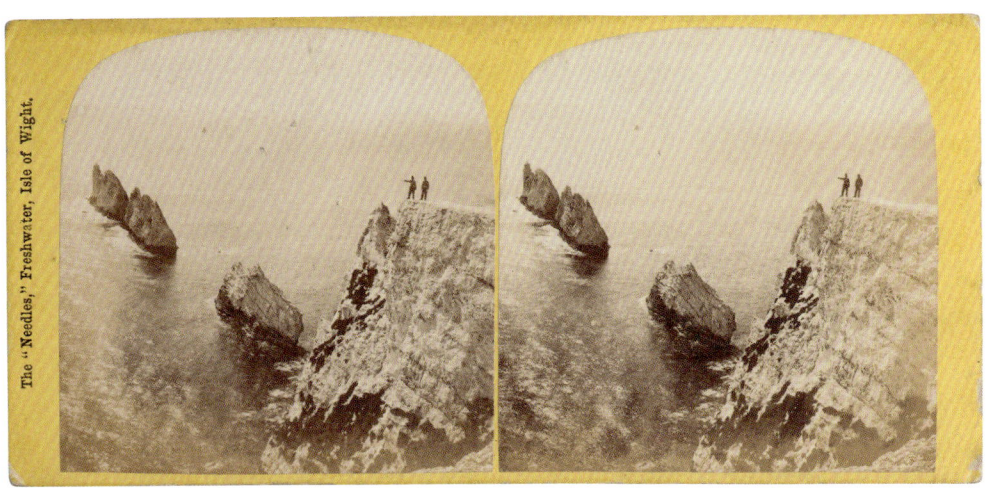

Stereoscopic photograph of the Needles

NETCC: 2016.909
Given by the family of Roy Brinton, 2016

The mid to late nineteenth century saw a craze for new photographic and optical technologies. These included stereoscopic photographs, composed of two images side by side which can be viewed through a special viewer to produce a single three-dimensional image. These became hugely popular with cards of various views sold at a range of prices and widely collected. Views such as this one of the Needles were a perfect souvenir for the Island's booming tourist market. This card was made by F. Hudson whose premises were in Ventnor High Street in 1865, and 2 Regent Parade, Mill Street between 1871 and 1875.

Sponsored by Dimbola Museum & Galleries

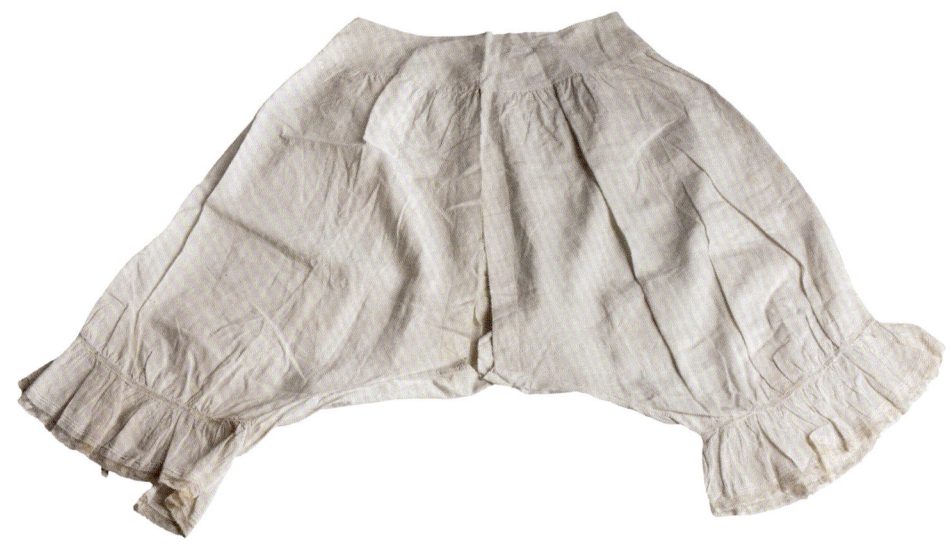

Princess Beatrice's drawers

NETCC: 2019.410
Given by Stephen Pinder, 2019

Following a long tradition, Queen Victoria gave clothes, including underwear, to her favourites and most faithful servants as a token of thanks. It is possible that her youngest daughter, Princess Beatrice, continued this practice and gave these drawers as a gift. They follow an older style of underwear formed of two separate legs and joined together at the waistband, leading to them often being called pairs. These drawers have been embroidered with Beatrice's royal monogram with the initials BB which indicates they were made after her marriage to Prince Henry of Battenberg.

Sponsored by Janet Tait and Jennifer Elford

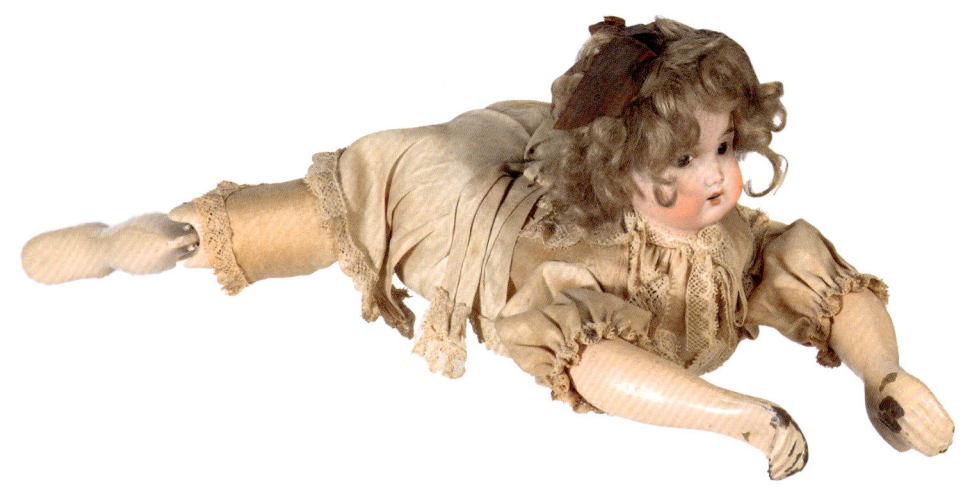

Clockwork swimming doll

NETCC: 1985.2720
Given by Miss J. Trask, 1959

This late nineteenth-century swimming doll uses a key-wound, spring-loaded mechanism to demonstrate the breaststroke. Made from porcelain, cork, wood and metal its head was made by the German company, Armand Marseille, one of the largest makers of doll heads in the world. The doll is wearing a Victorian swimming costume and was intended to teach children how to swim, although it could not be used in the water. Mechanical swimming dolls may have been invented by Frenchman 'Martin' who exhibited one at the 1879 'Exposition Universelle' in Paris.

Sponsored by Jennifer Culshaw

Doll's house

NETCC: 1985.2779
Given by Edith E. Marriott, 1968

This Victorian doll's house was donated to the museum in the 1960s and has been on display for many years becoming a familiar sight for visitors. It was owned by the donor's aunt whose father made it from a cupboard in the 1870s. The contents were collected and added to by the family over the years and the house is furnished with incredible detail. It features all the home comforts of an affluent family. There is a miniature four-poster bed, drawers that contain doll-sized items of clothing, a cabinet filled with tiny shells collected from Colwell Bay, carved bone candlesticks from Switzerland that hold real candles, a Welsh dresser displays the family's best china and a small metal photo album contains minuscule photographs of the donor's family.

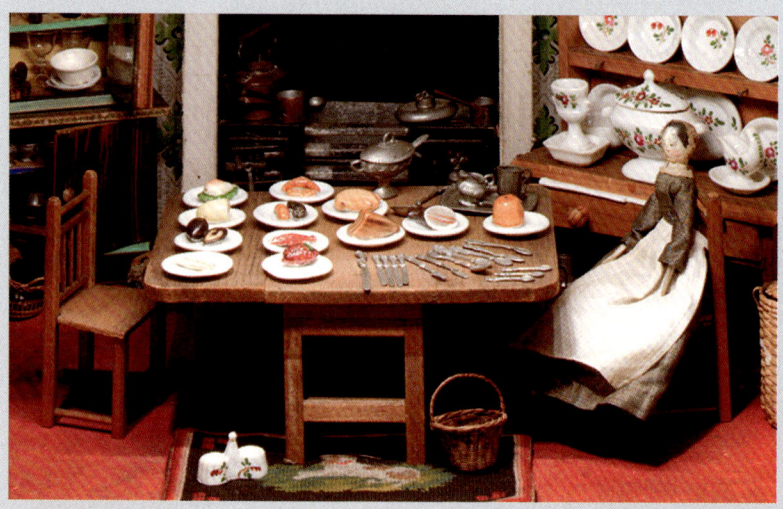

Sponsored by Clairey Meadowcroft

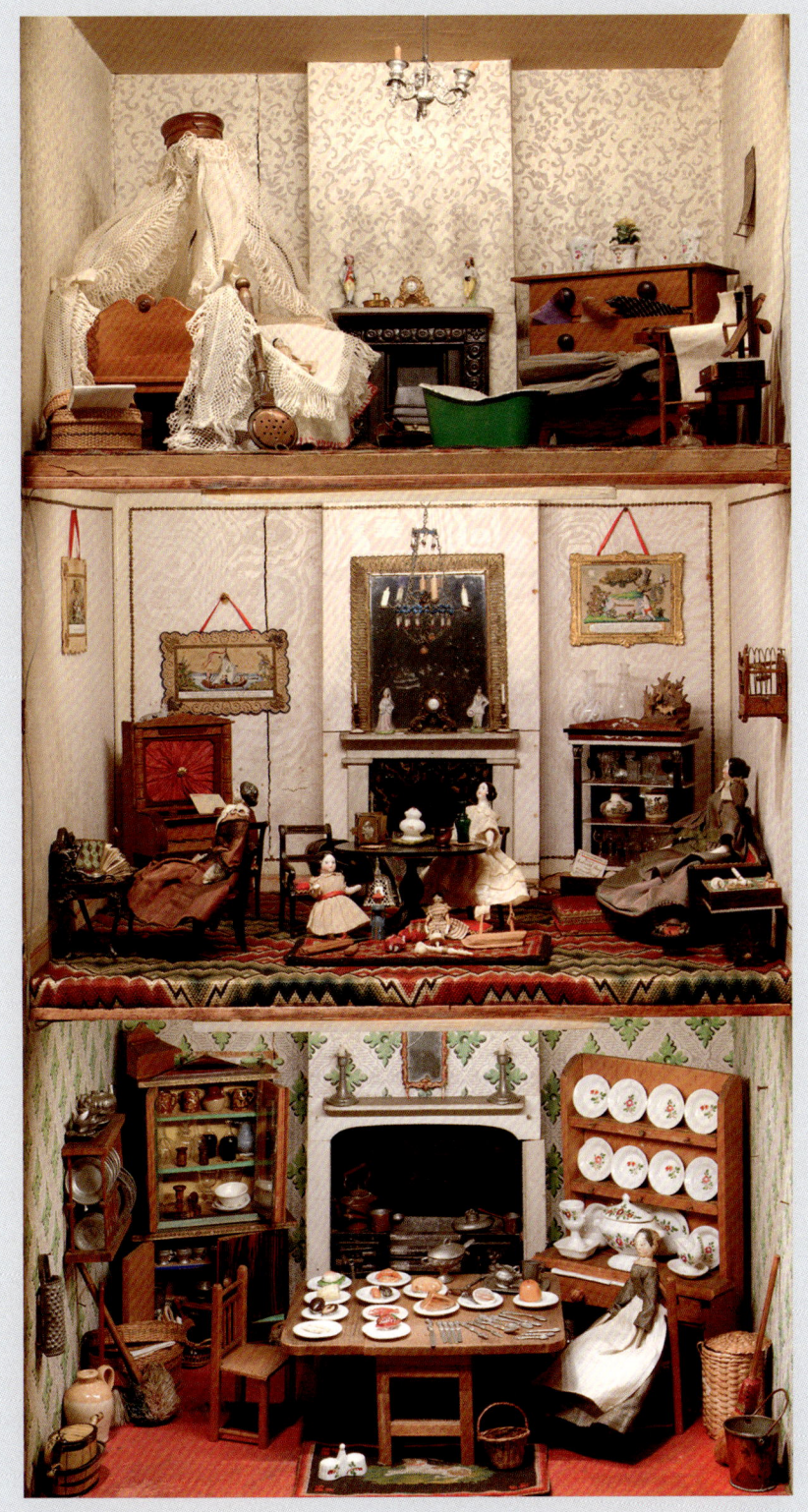

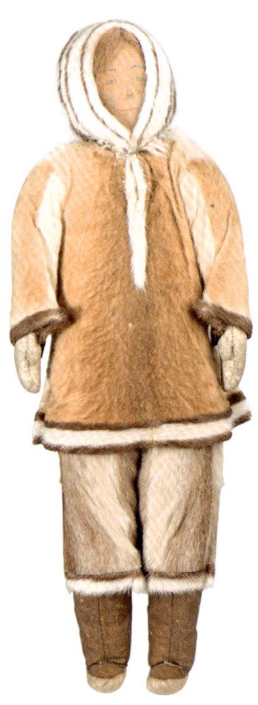

Inuit doll made in Lapland

NETCC: 1985.2721
Given by M.A. Alderslade, 1964

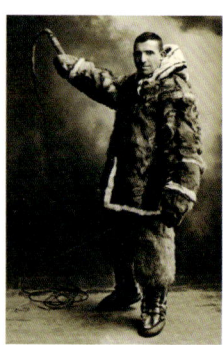

Edgar Greenshield wearing Inuit clothing.
NETCC: 1985.2721.2

Edgar Greenshield (1877-1938) was the son of a Newport draper and at the age of 20 joined the Church Missionary Society college where he learnt medical and technical skills as well as theology. In 1901, he set sail on his first mission to the Canadian Arctic where he endured violent snowstorms, freezing temperatures and long hours of darkness. On several trips to Blacklead Island, he learnt to speak the Inuit language and put his medical and practical skills to use.

He was given a doll by 14-year-old Mollie Alderslade of Newport, to present to an Inuit girl. When he returned home, he brought with him a hand-made doll from the Inuit girl, Ahnerkkoo, to thank Mollie and return the favour. The doll's head is made from driftwood, its outfit is from caribou skin and the hair is from a musk ox. The leather for the footwear was chewed by elderly ladies to soften it up before cutting and sewing. It was used in a Newport school to teach geography.

Sponsored by Ian and Marie Robertson

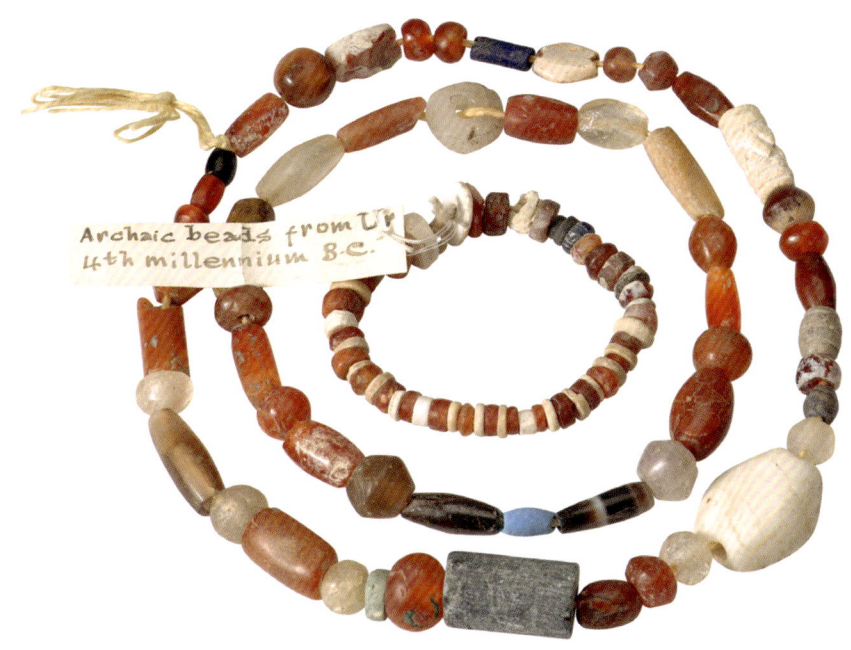

Beads from Ur

NETCC: 1985.5468

Excavated from one of the earliest graves at Ur, an ancient city located between modern-day Iran and Iraq, these beads date to around 3500- 3300 BCE. They were given to Catherine Morey, an early curator of the Museum, by C. L. Woolley of the British Museum, in gratitude for the financial contributions she made to the dig. Woolley uncovered about 1,850 burials, including 16 described as royal tombs and containing many valuable artefacts. He later wrote extensively about these discoveries attracting attention and visitors to the ruins. One of these visitors was Agatha Christie, who married one of Woolley's assistants and wrote 'Murder in Mesopotamia', inspired by the discovery of the tombs.

These beads are an example of how a diverse range of objects have found their way, via various routes, into the collection over the Museum's long history.

Sponsored by Mary Flynn

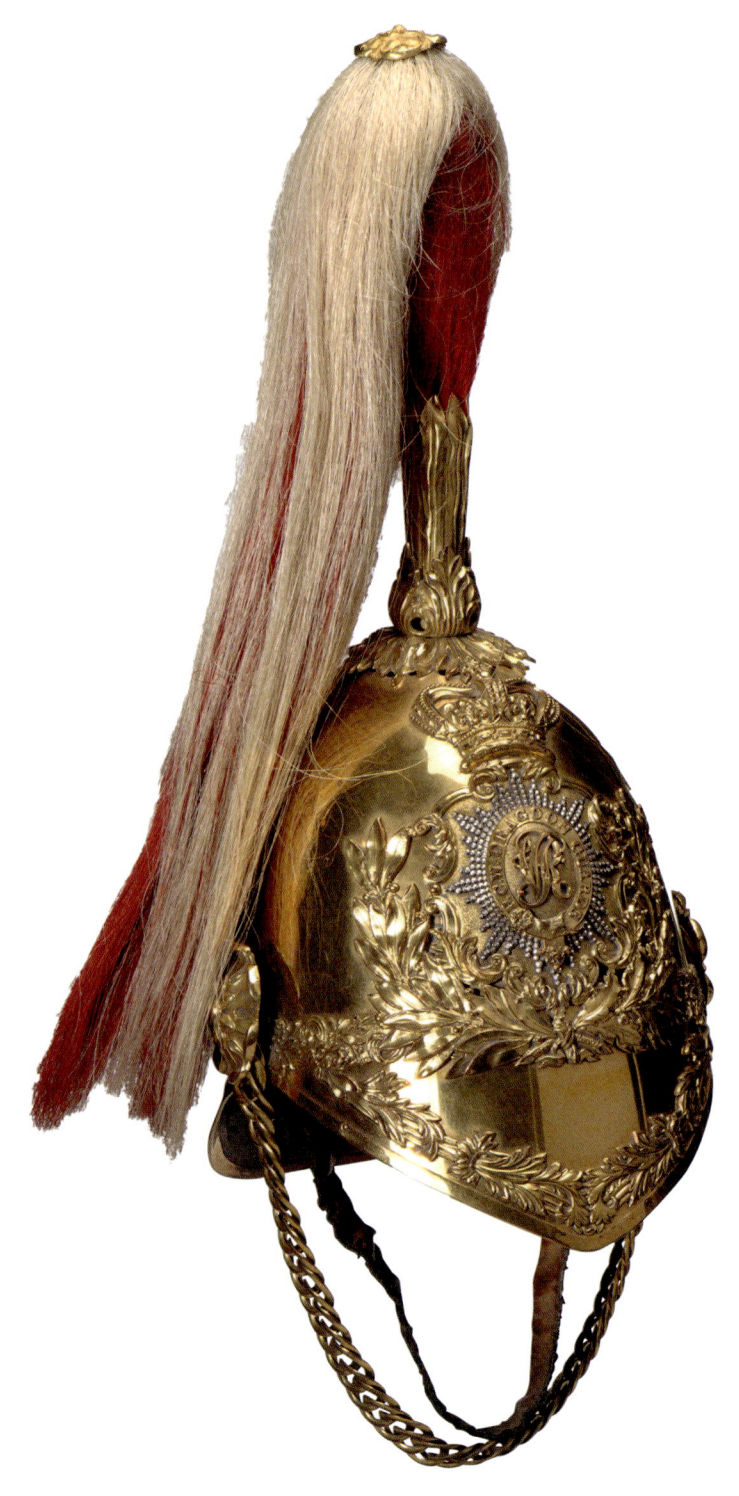

Somerset John Gough-Calthorpe's Dragoon Guards Helmet

NECTC: 1985.3513 L
Lent by Lady Elizabeth Calthorpe

Lieut-General Somerset John Gough-Calthorpe (1831–1912) was a decorated British officer and politician who travelled all over the world. During the Crimean War, he served as aide-de-camp to Lord Raglan and later published a memoir of the war including his eyewitness account of the Charge of the Light Brigade. His account of the decisions of Lord Cardigan led to Cardigan suing him for libel, although the case never came to trial.

Somerset John was promoted to Lieutenant-Colonel in 1861 and commanded the mounted 5th Dragoon Guards before retiring to Woodlands Vale in Ryde in 1869. He was the first Chairman of the Isle of Wight Council from 1890 to 1898 and also served as a Justice of the Peace. The Lady Chapel at St John's Church in Oakfield near Ryde was built as a memorial to him in 1914.

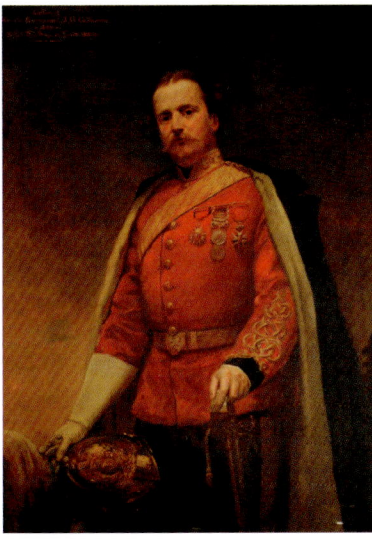

Somerset John Gough Calthorpe, 1869
(Courtesy of Lady Elizabeth Calthorpe)

Japanese Aikuchi

NETCC: 1985.1619 L
Lent by Lady Elizabeth Calthorpe

All of the ivories in our collection are antiques. Trade in ivory was banned in 1989 by the United Nations Convention on International Trade in Endangered Species of Wild Fauna and Flora (CITES), to help protect endangered species, particularly elephants.

This carved ivory dagger was bought by Admiral Somerset Arthur Gough-Calthorpe (1864-1937) in Japan in 1892 and given to his father, Lieut. General Somerset John Gough-Calthorpe, an avid collector of weapons and campaign souvenirs. The dagger is of a type known as an aikuchi and while the handle and scabbard are finely carved, the quality of the blade suggests it may have been made for the European market. A small utility knife, called a Kozuka, fits into a pocket on the scabbard.

Despite being born into a celebrated army family, Somerset Arthur joined the navy in 1878. A senior British Admiral during World War One, he served as commander-in-chief in the Mediterranean signing the Armistice of Mudros on behalf of the Allies. After the war, he became a Deputy Lieutenant for the Isle of Wight and lived at Woodlands Vale in Ryde.

Sponsored by Lady Elizabeth Calthorpe

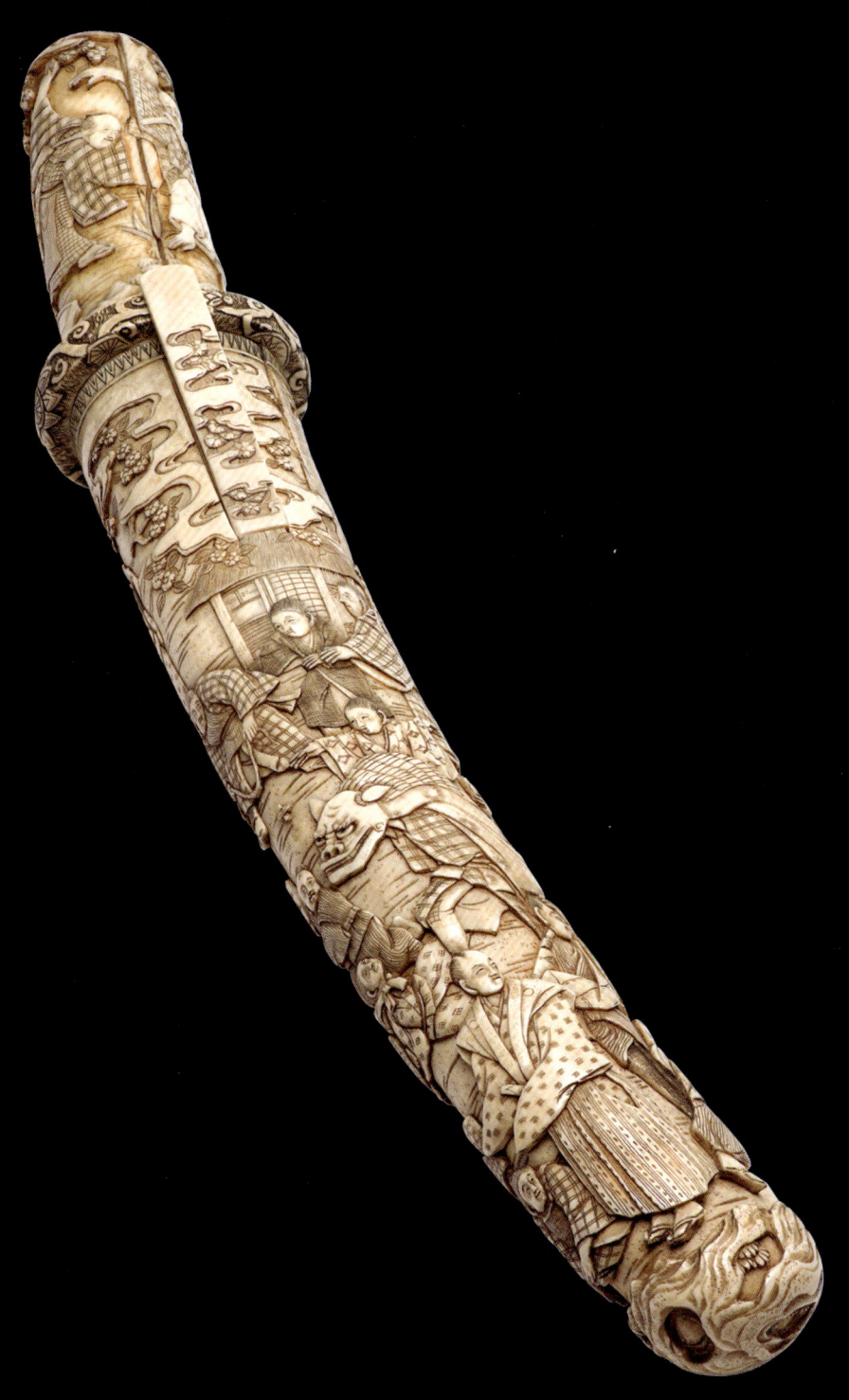

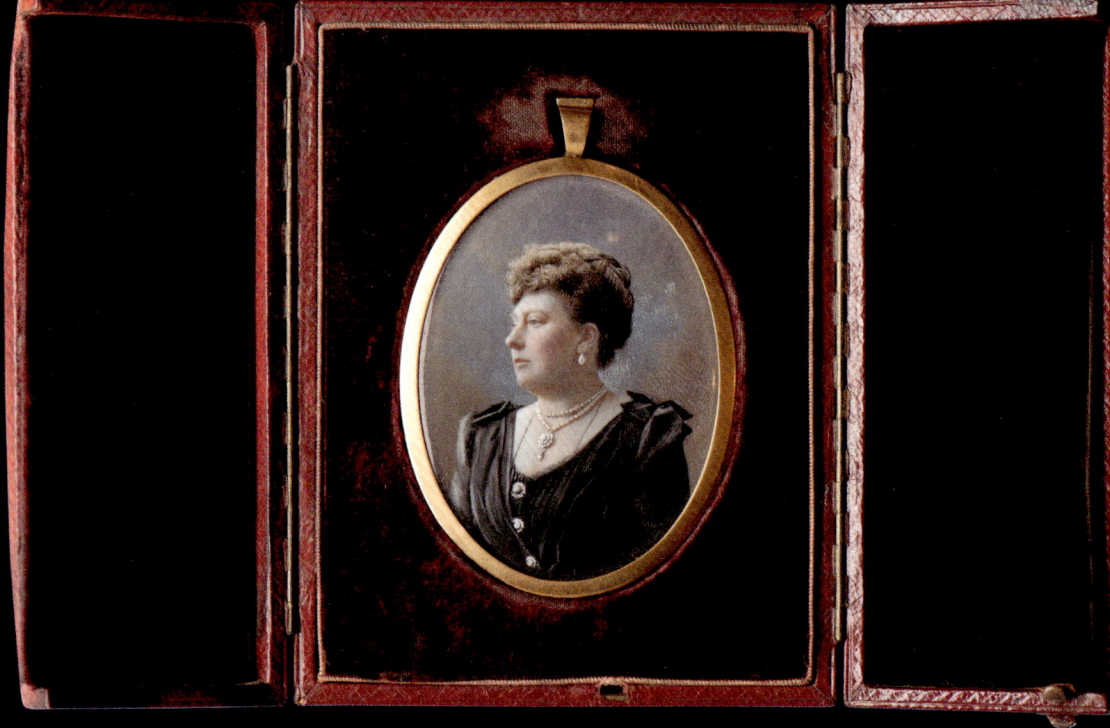

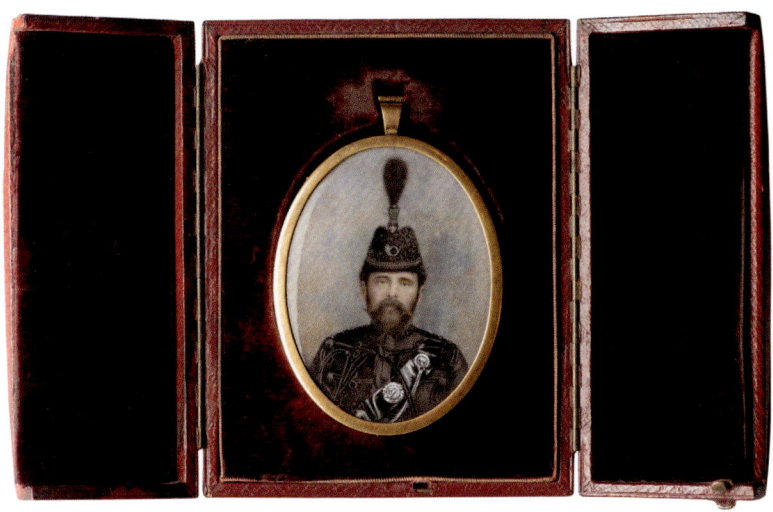

Miniature portraits of Prince Henry and Princess Beatrice

NETCC: P.1986.2140
Given by the Isle of Wight Rifles Trust, 1967

The youngest of Queen Victoria's children, Princess Beatrice was intended to be her mother's companion and secretary and never to marry. But while attending the wedding of her niece, Princess Victoria of Hesse and by Rhine, at Darmstadt, Beatrice fell in love with the groom's brother, Prince Henry of Battenberg. When Beatrice told her mother of her intention to marry, the Queen was so angry she refused to speak to her daughter for months, communicating only by note. She finally agreed on the condition that the couple live with her so Beatrice could continue to support her mother. The couple were married at Saint Mildred's Church at Whippingham, near Osborne House where a private suite was created for them. This watercolour double portrait was presented to the officer's mess of the Isle of Wight Rifles by Colonel E.W. Cradock in 1896, the year of Prince Henry's death.

Sponsored by Anne Longford DL

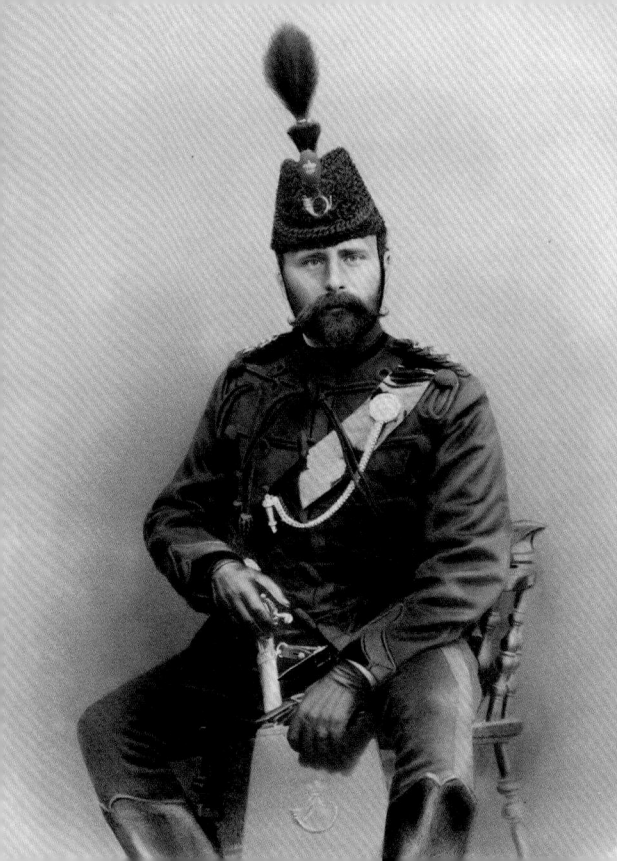

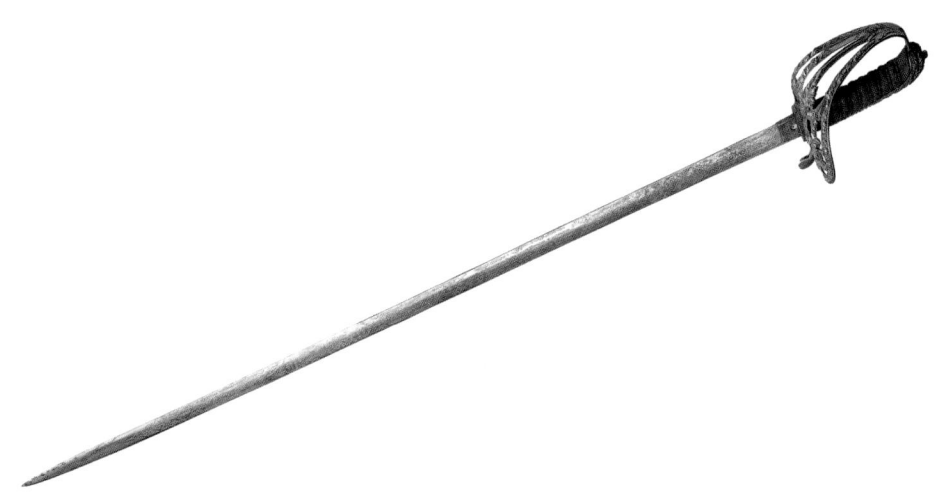

Prince Henry's Isle of Wight Rifles sword

NETCC: 1985.1605

Given by the Marquess of Carisbrooke, 1945

This ceremonial sword was presented to Prince Henry by the officers of the Isle of Wight Rifles when he was appointed the regiment's first Honorary Colonel upon his marriage to Princess Beatrice in July 1885, the same year as the regiment was renamed 'The 5th Isle of Wight, Princess Beatrice's Volunteer Battalion of the Hampshire Regiment'. Henry performed his duties with great enthusiasm and took part in several field days and marches.

In 1895, Henry accompanied an expeditionary force to the Gold Coast of West Africa, modern-day Ghana. The men were to fight in the 4th Anglo-Ashanti War between British colonial powers who wanted to establish complete control of the area and its gold, and the Ashanti Empire who refused to surrender their sovereignty. Not long after the troops arrived malaria broke out in the camp and Henry fell ill. He never made it home, dying on board HMS Blonde on January 20th, 1896. A letter containing his last wishes gave the sword to the regiment and asked that future Colonels wear it during regimental inspections.

Sponsored by Brigadier Maurice Sheen CBE QVRM TD DL, HM Vice Lord-Lieutenant of the Isle of Wight, in memory of his uncle, Bugler Albert Edward Downer of Calbourne who was killed in action at Gallipoli on 31 October 1915 whilst serving with The Isle of Wight Rifles.

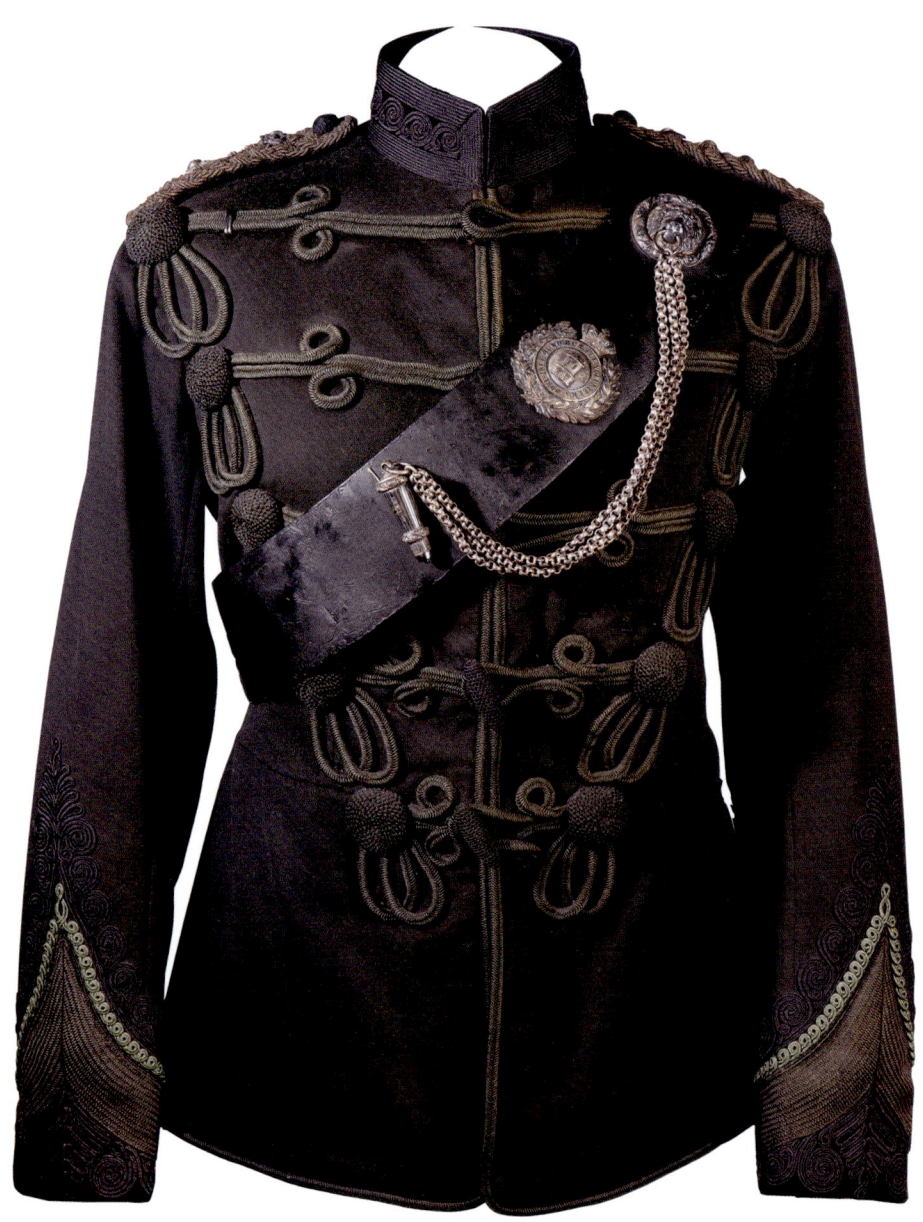

George V's Isle of Wight Rifles jacket

NETCC: 1985.3540

Founded in 1860 for home defence, the Isle of Wight Rifles were a volunteer corps and territorial unit made up of local men who were not regular soldiers. This green woollen uniform jacket was worn by their Honorary Colonel, the Duke of York, Princess Beatrice's nephew, and later George V. He had succeeded Beatrice's late husband Prince Henry at a special ceremony at Osborne House in 1897. Upon his accession to the throne, George became Colonel-in-Chief of the regiment and his connection helped raise new recruits prior to the outbreak of the First World War.

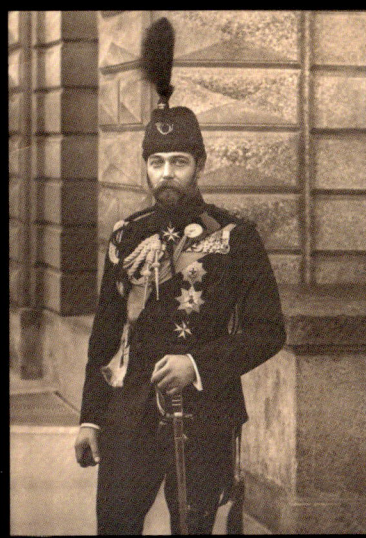

George V in the uniform of the Isle of Wight Rifles
NETCC: P.1986.2112

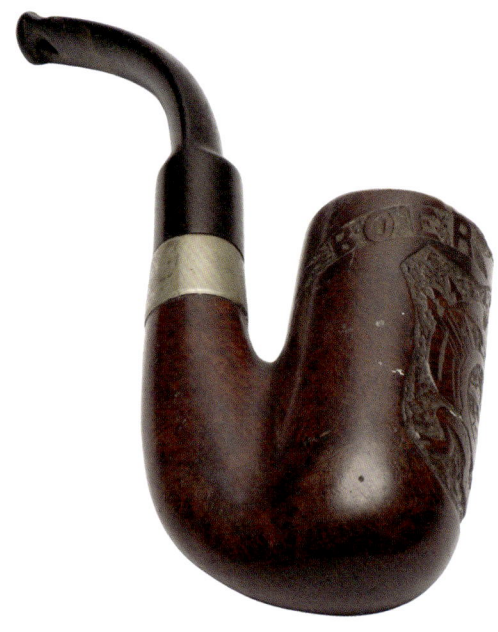

Frederick Nobbs' Boer War pipe

NETCC: 2022.71

Given by Claire Nobbs in memory of Brian Graham Nobbs, 2022

Frederick Nobbs (1882-1963) was the eldest of 15 children and lived on Harts Lane in Rookley. In 1900 when he was just 18, he sailed from Southampton on the troop ship 'Orotava' to fight in the Boer War. From Pretoria in 1900 he wrote to his mother: "Dear Mother I am pleased to tell you that I have received the paper every week ... there is always seven or eight around me for to have a look at the County Press." This briar pipe is carved with the coat of arms of The South African Republic, also known as the Transvaal Republic. Pipes like this were often carved by Boer prisoners of war. Frederick stayed in South Africa until the war ended in 1902 and returned to the Isle of Wight with the pipe as a souvenir.

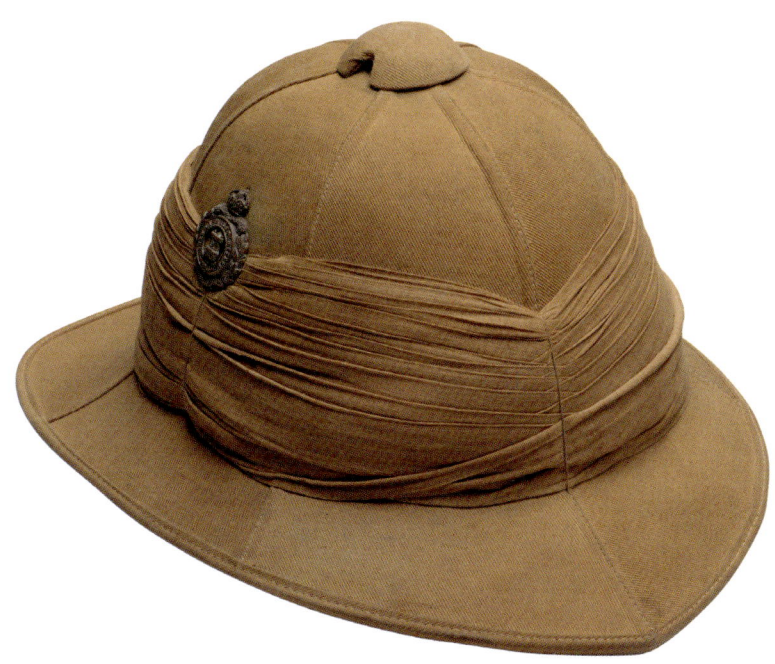

World War One pith helmet

NETCC: 2019.492
Given by Anne Fraser, 2019

Pith helmets are lightweight cloth-covered helmets worn to protect the head and face from the sun. They were widely used by troops fighting in the Middle East and Africa during World War One. This helmet belonged to W. Anthony who served in the Isle of Wight Rifles in 1915.

Landing at Gallipoli in August 1915, the Rifles intended to help British, French and Commonwealth troops drive back Turkish forces but the peninsular was well defended and they suffered very heavy losses. By September, having suffered 50% casualties, the battalion was moved back to Anzac Cove and in November was evacuated to Egypt. From here they joined the offensive in Palestine, where they remained until the final defeat of the Turkish army at the end of 1918.

Sponsored for Derek Warman

Private Archibald Warren's World War One memorial plaque

NETCC: 1989.152

Given by D. Jolliffe, 1989

Archie served in the 2nd Battalion Hampshire Regiment and was one of eight brothers from Ventnor who all signed up to fight in the war. In 1915 the Isle of Wight Mercury reported his enlistment, the last brother to do so, noting of his mother that "we doubt if in the Isle of Wight and immediate district any mother can point to such a proud record." The three youngest boys were all killed in action - Archie died in Belgium in August 1917, Edgar in Palestine in April 1917, and Reuben in Belgium in June 1915.

In 1916 it was decided that some kind of memorial should be given to the next of kin of those who died. A bronze plaque which commonly became known as a 'dead man's penny' was designed and by 1920 over 1.3 million had been issued. Around the edge, it reads: "He Died for Freedom and Honour."

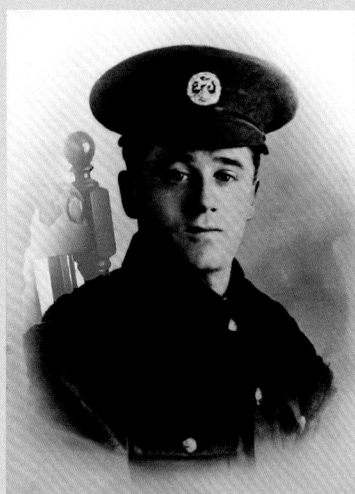

Archie Warren in uniform
NETCC: 1989.145

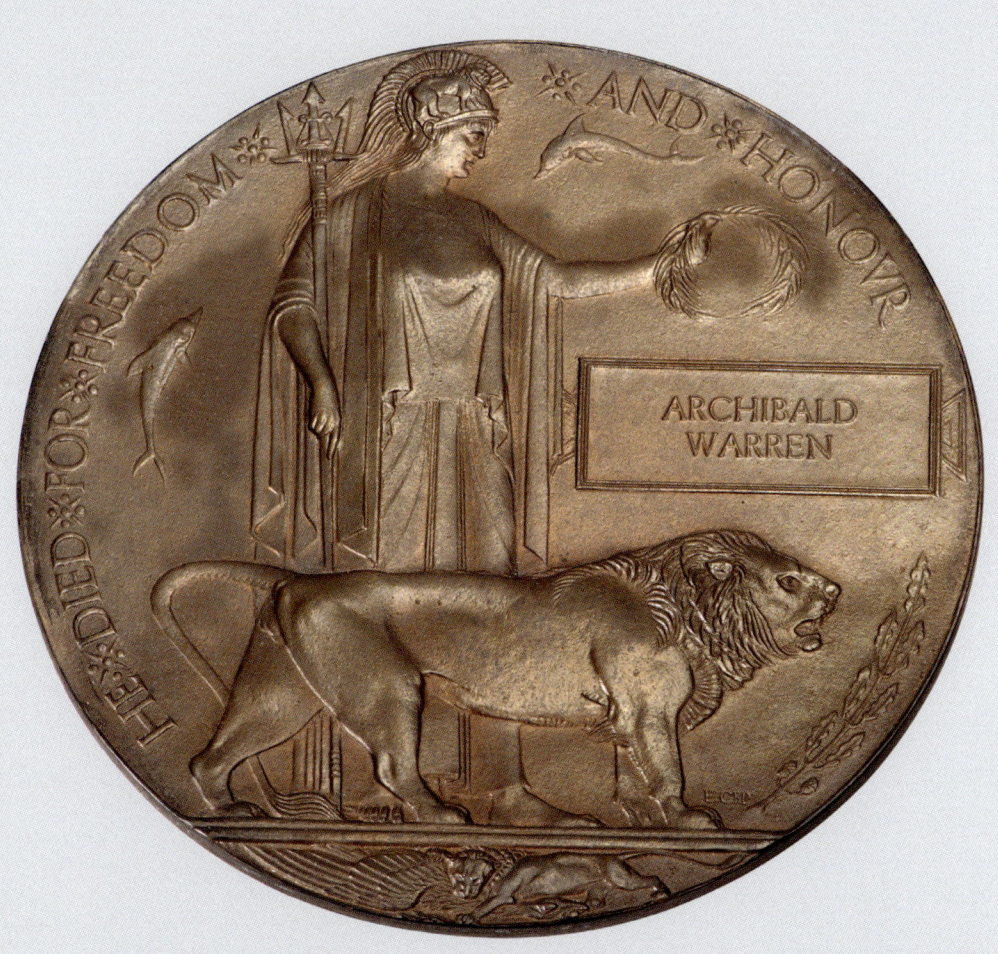

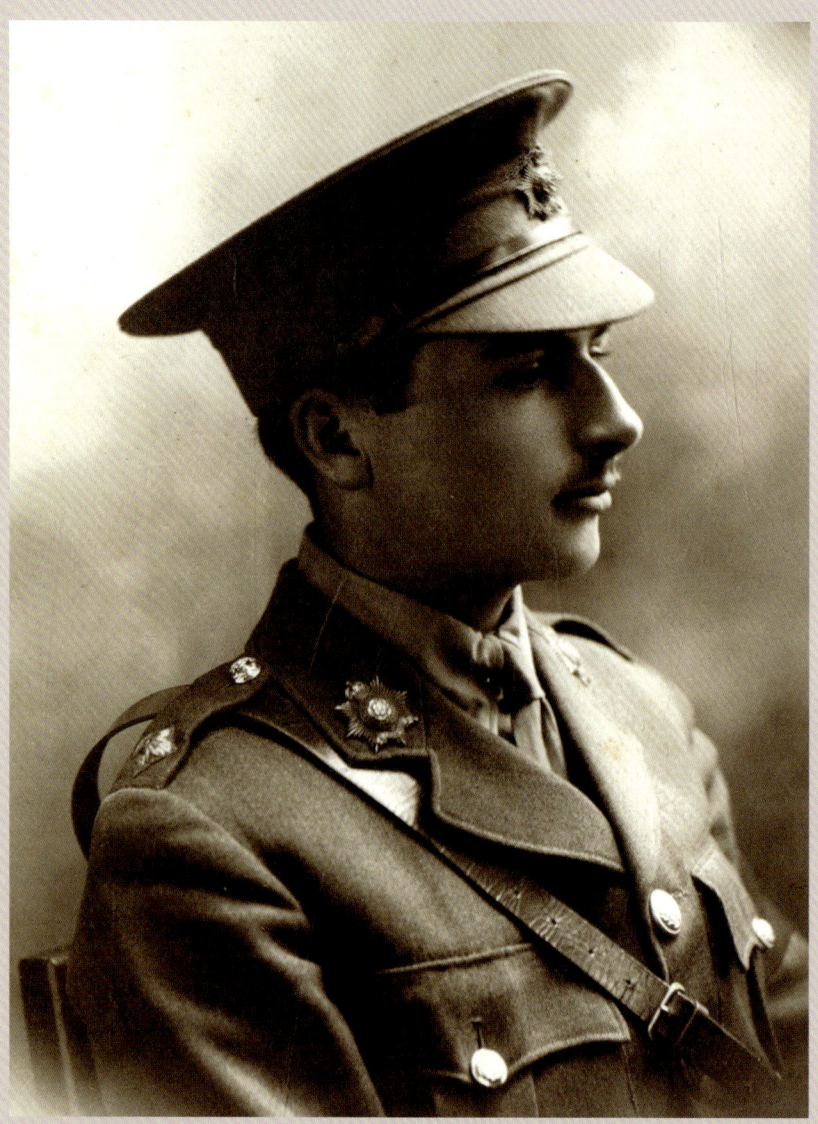

Lieutenant Reginald Denham, 1917
NETCC: 1996.73

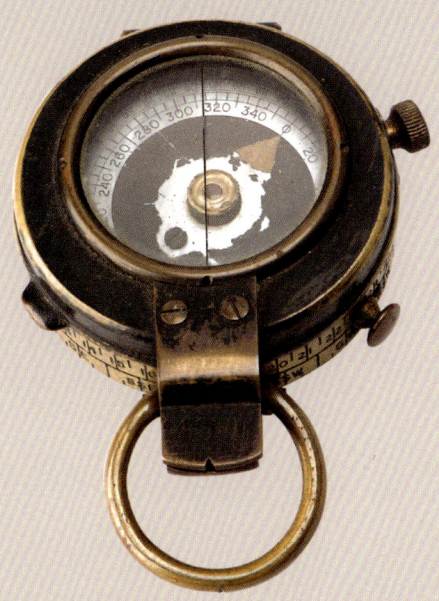

Lieut. Reginald Denham's World War One compass

NETCC: 2017.45
Given by John Denham, 2014

Reg was born in 1895 and attended Newport Grammar School where he excelled at cricket, won the prestigious Kings Prize and became Head Boy. He worked at the County Asylum, Whitecroft, before enlisting in the 1st Royal Army Medical Corp Territorials in 1914. He was stationed at Southsea General Hospital before transferring to the 2nd Wiltshire Regiment in France in 1916.

In letters to his mother, he wrote: "We work all night & sleep by day so you can guess we do not know the date or the day of the week... Trench life is quite an experience & what with dodging whizzbangs & keeping rats out of your dug out you are well occupied... My word we have some specimens of rats out here. They fight just like cats & make an awful row... I shall be back like a bad egg one of these fine days. So cheer up ma." Reg was killed in 1918 while withdrawing under German fire.

Sponsored by Lin Watterson who published his WW1 letters to his family

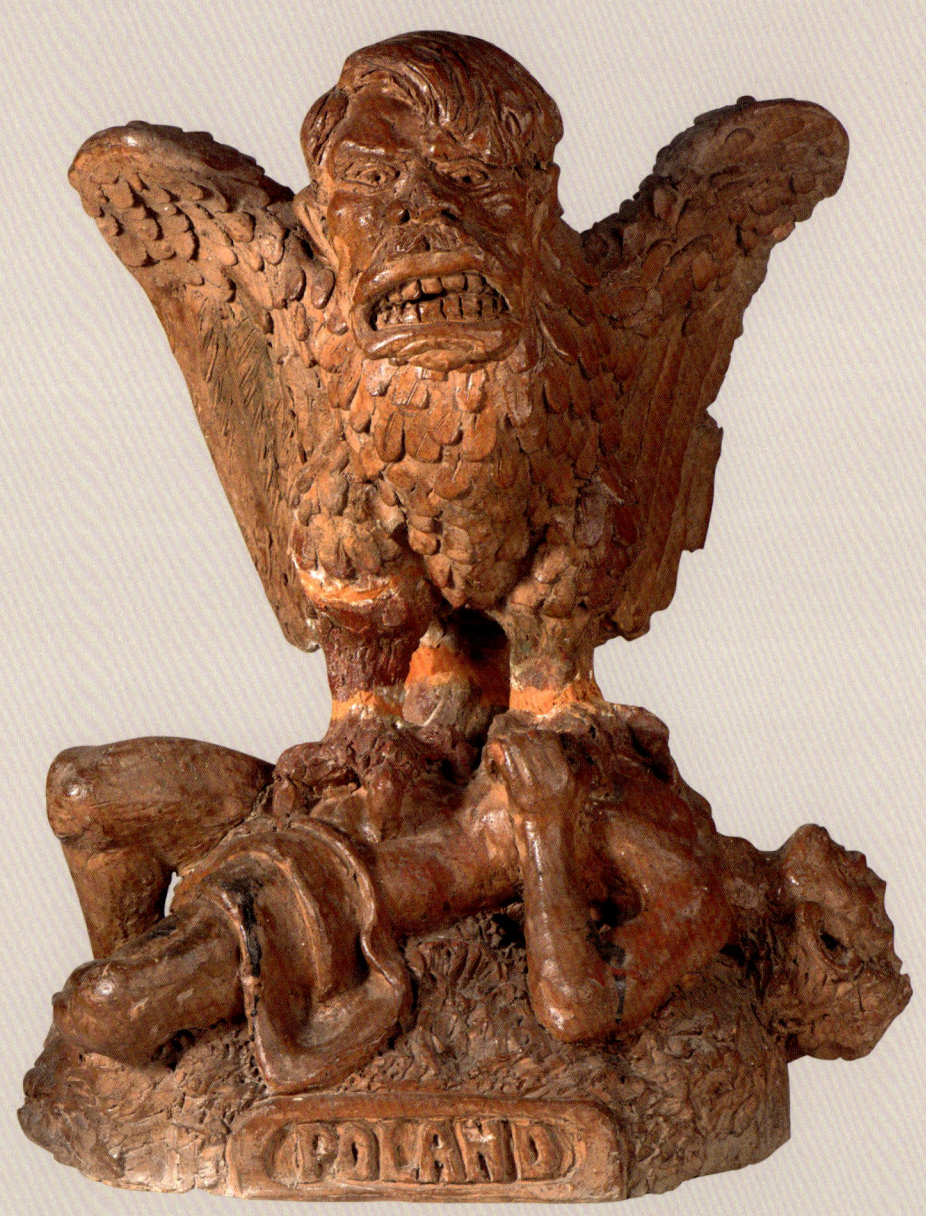

Terracotta caricature of Hitler

NETCC: 2015.90
Given by the Estate of Audrey Russell, 2015

This unusual terracotta figure was commissioned by Roy Russell of Stenbury Manor, near Godshill, during the Second World War. It depicts an eagle with the caricatured face of Adolf Hitler, sinking its talons into a corpse symbolising Poland, a political comment on the invasion of that country by Nazi forces. It was made by Harry Pritchett (1875-1954) the son of a brickmaker who created skilful and imaginative terracotta sculptures and ornaments, many of which decorate Isle of Wight buildings to this day.

Harry first entered the family business, the 'Hillis Brick and Tile Works' in Cowes, when he was 19. He practised modelling clay while filling spare hours at the brickyard. Initially working for the family business and later from his studio - a shed in his garden - his work ranged from decorative terracotta wares and sculpture to building enrichments such as roof terminals and plaques. His feeling for the grotesque and his experience creating gargoyles are apparent in this strange sculpture.

Sponsored by Ian and Claire Wellby

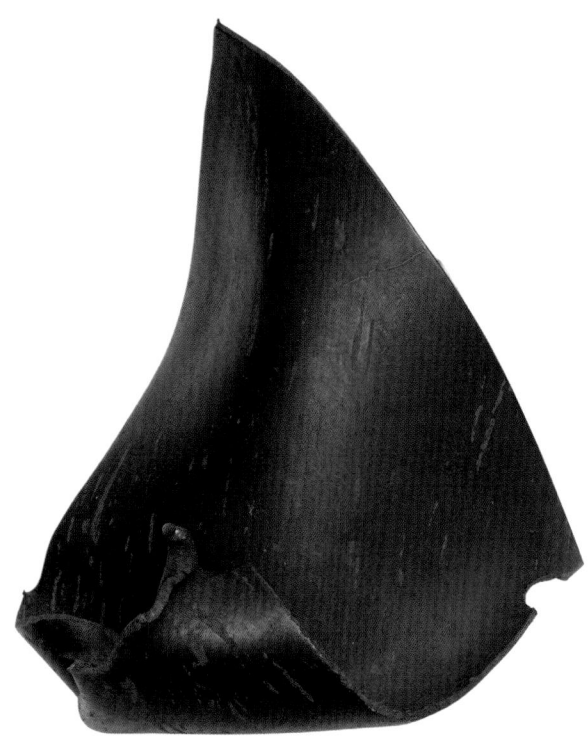

World War Two shrapnel

NETCC: 1985.1488
Given by C.T. Rayner, 1981

This fragment of bomb casing was kept as a souvenir after it fell in front of Beach Cottage in Shanklin on October 13th, 1942. Between 1940 and 1944, there were 125 bombing attacks on the Isle of Wight damaging over 10,000 buildings and killing 214 people. The Island was not only on the route for Luftwaffe bombers travelling to the major ports of Portsmouth and Southampton but was also a target for bombing itself due to the shipbuilding and aircraft industries at Cowes and East Cowes and the radar station on the downs above Ventnor. One of the most dramatic incidents during the war came on the night of May 4th to 5th, 1942, when the Polish destroyer ORP Błyskawica, which was at the J.S. White's shipyard for an emergency refit, defended the towns of Cowes and East Cowes from an attack by a detachment of 160 bombers.

Sponsored by Mark Saunders

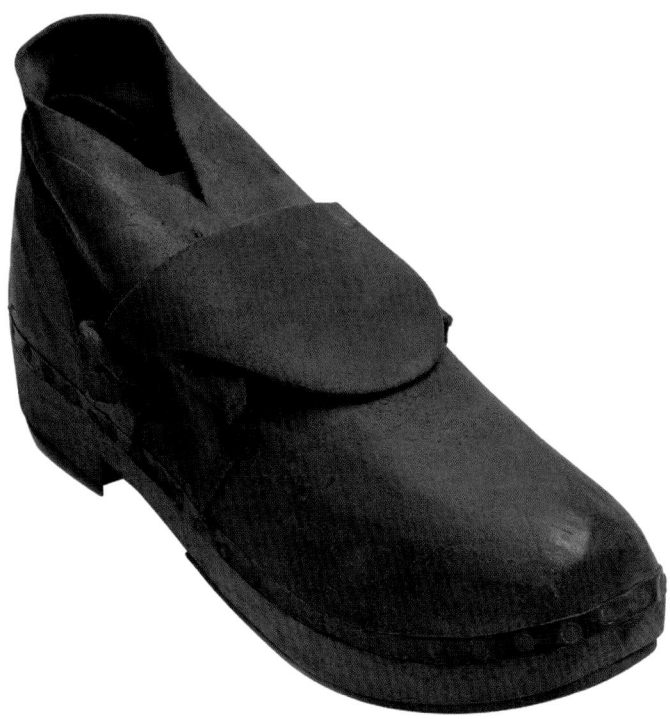

Shipyard clog

NETCC: 1991.318
Given by D. Jolliffe, 1989

This leather and wood clog was designed to be worn by factory workers. A thick leather tab and wooden sole protect the foot from molten metal and other hazards. It came from the stockroom of Jolliffe's shoe shop in Cowes and probably dates to the Second World War when the town, and East Cowes across the River Medina, were centres of military ship and aircraft production. Between 1938 and 1945 nearly 50 naval vessels were built at J. S. White's in Cowes, and around 6,000 people were employed making aircraft at Saunders-Roe in East Cowes at this time.

Sponsored for Stephen and Elaine Griffiths

Pair of ladies' python skin shoes

NETCC: 1991.314
Given by Gladys Jolliffe, 1991

These python skin shoes date from the 1940s and bear a 'utility mark', in accordance with a wartime government scheme introduced to make the production of civilian clothing more efficient and provide price- regulated quality clothing. Wartime shortages forced manufacturers to be inventive with their use of materials. Snake, lizard and crocodile skins had been popular in the 1920s, and a surplus of the material after it fell out of fashion led to its later use in these, a particularly stylish example of utility clothing.

They are from the stockroom of H. Jolliffe and Sons, a fashionable boot and shoe retailer first opened in Cowes in 1853 by Mr Henry Jolliffe. The business passed through 3 more generations of the family until it finally closed in 1991 with the retirement of Gladys Jolliffe, Henry's great-granddaughter. At this time the museum was invited to select items from the shop's stockroom, the contents of which had been accrued over its more than 130 years in business.

Sponsored by Vectis Forties Vintage (V4V)

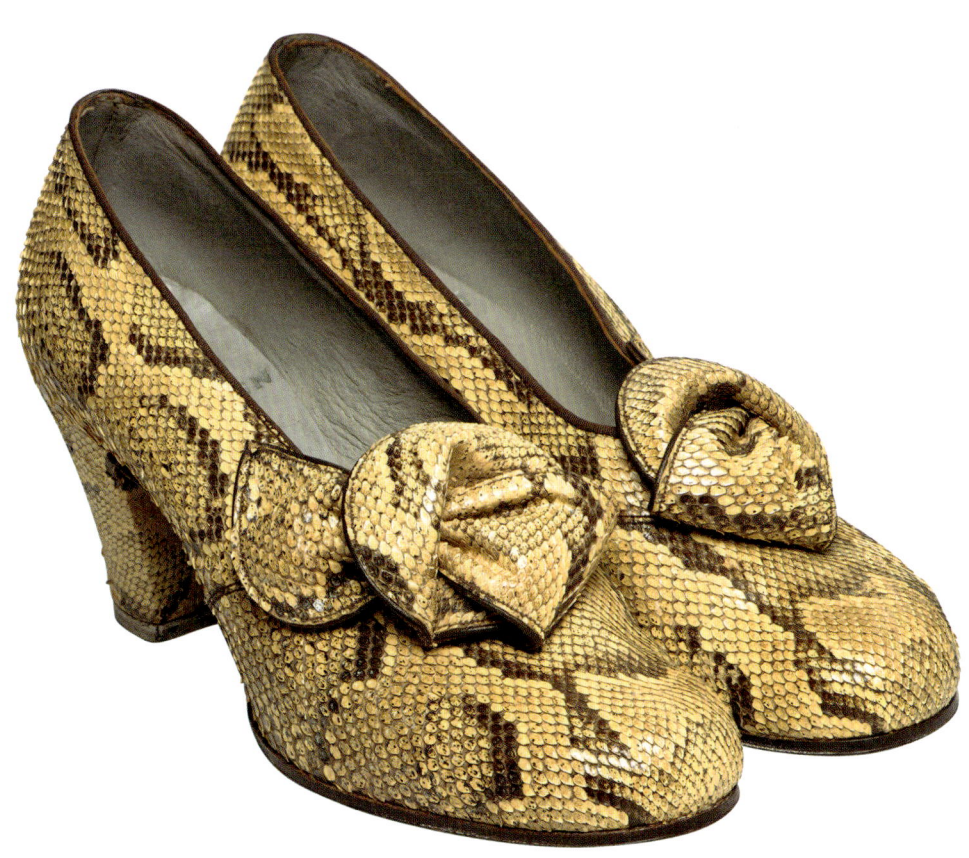

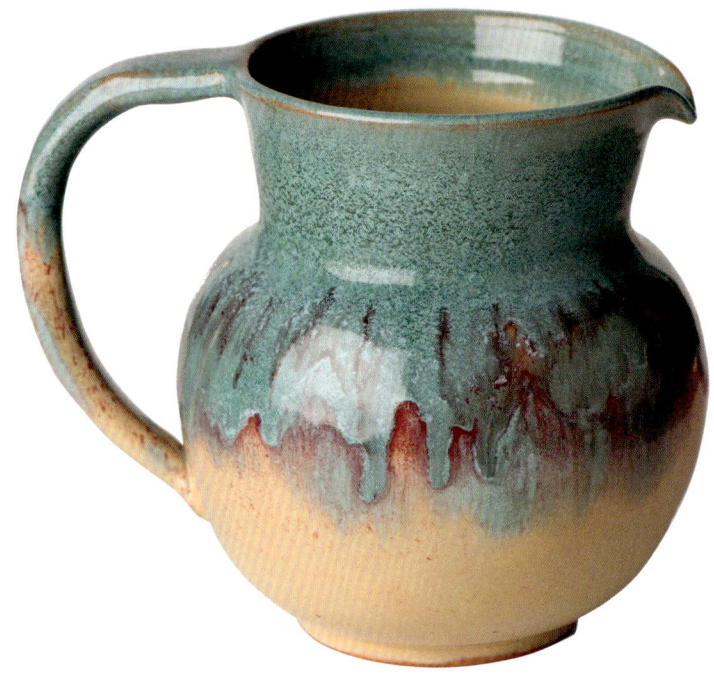

Isle of Wight Handcraft Pottery

NETCC: 1985.4022
Purchased, 1983

The Isle of Wight Handcraft Pottery was established in 1926 by local entrepreneur Samuel Edgar Saunders. Throughout the 1920s and 30s, it used locally sourced clay to produce hand-thrown domestic earthenware. Many of the wares made in the 1930s feature a distinctive high-gloss glaze in mottled and streaked shades of turquoise, green and blue often with pink tinges, which was allowed to drip down the vessel. Manager Edward Bagley carried a secret recipe book of glaze mixtures. Although the pottery operated for almost 12 years and its wares were extremely popular, it never made a sustained profit and finally closed in February 1938.

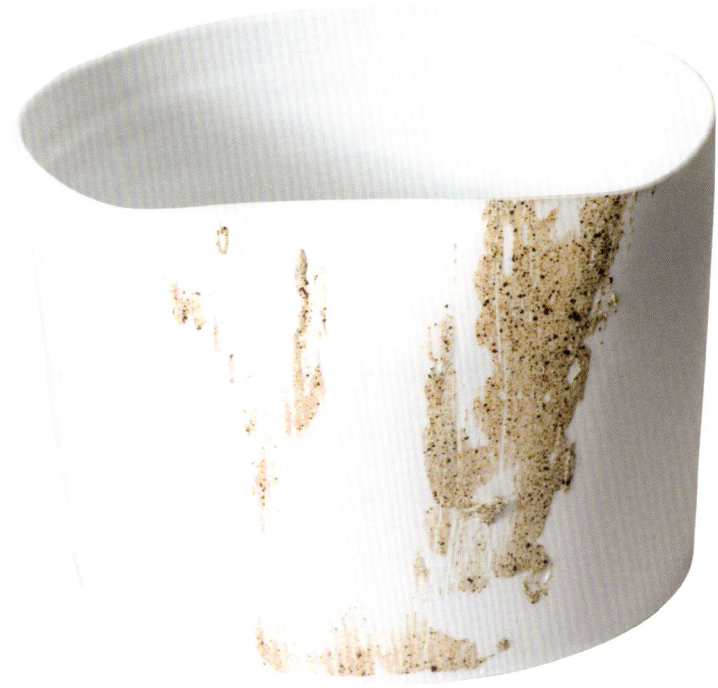

Ceramic vessel

NETCC: 2021.82
Given by Sue Paraskeva, 2021

Created by ceramic artist Sue Paraskeva in 2004, this cylindrical porcelain vessel is decorated with local wood slip. From her studio in Ryde, Sue specialises in the hand production of finely thrown porcelain, combining traditional methods with experimental forms and firing techniques. She produces one-off pieces alongside gallery and public space installation work and a tableware range. Her refined aesthetic is sought after by consumers and collectors all over the world. Sue's prestigious clientele includes Kevin Costner, Calvin Klein and Tom Kerridge and her work is held in both private and public collections.

Sponsored by Sue Bennett

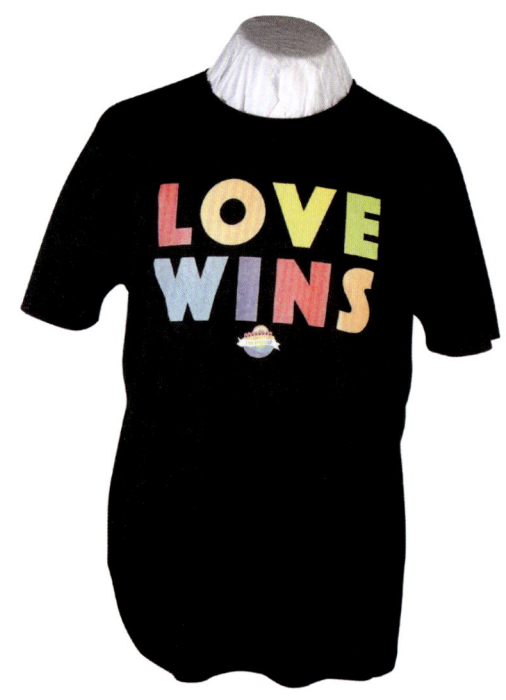

Love Wins t-shirt

NETCC: 2017.475
Given by Yve White, 2018

In late 2016 a small team of volunteers decided to organise the Isle of Wight's first-ever Pride event. Over 4,000 people attended Pride in 2017, bringing the parade cheerfully through the town and down to the beach where speakers and entertainers performed throughout the day. Afterwards, the organisers said: "It was amazing to see people of all backgrounds, of all ages and of all sexualities coming together and celebrating Love."

This t-shirt was manufactured by Isle of Wight firm, Rapanui. It was founded by two brothers Rob and Mart Drake-Knight in 2007, and it now employs over 80 people full-time on the Island, at Rapanui and its print-on-demand platform, Teemill. Rapanui products are printed to order and made from organic cotton using renewable energy. Each item is designed to be sent back when worn out so that Rapanui can make new products from the recovered material.

Sponsored by StoneCrabs Theatre

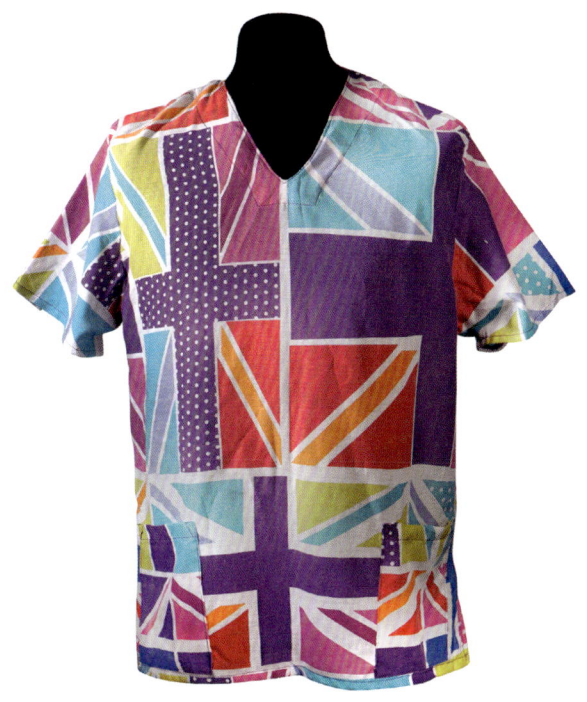

Home-made scrubs

NETCC: 2021.1
Given by Nikki Morris, 2020

These medical scrubs were made by one of the Isle of Wight 'For the Love of Scrubs' volunteers during the Covid-19 pandemic. Throughout the country, sewers responded to the desperate need for scrubs as supplies of PPE ran short. Members of the public were asked to donate fabric, in particular sheets and duvet covers made of polycotton which could be washed at 60 degrees to kill the Covid virus. These were used to create the scrubs that were given to care homes and other healthcare providers.

On the Island 190 volunteers from 12 to over 80 years old contributed by not only sewing and pattern cutting, but by making deliveries and organising the group's efforts. As the need for scrubs began to lessen, the museum approached the group and asked them to donate some to our collection in the hope that aspects of what happened during the pandemic, and our local communities' response to it, could be captured for future generations.

Sponsored by Richard and Ann Smout

Further Reading

- Arnold, C. J., The Anglo-Saxon cemeteries of the Isle of Wight (1982)
- Brinton, Roy, Isle of Wight, The Complete Guide (2006)
- Dennison, Matthew, The Last Princess, The Devoted Life of Queen Victoria's Youngest Daughter (2007)
- Dowden, Andrew and Lisa, A Century of Ceramics: A Selection of 20th Century Potters and Potteries in the Isle of Wight (2005)
- Jones, Jack D., The Royal Prisoner (1965)
- Jones, Jack D., Isle of Wight Curiosities, A Guide to Follies, Curious Tales, Unusual People and Architectural Eccentricities (1992)
- Jones, Jack and Johanna, The Isle of Wight, An Illustrated History (1987)
- Jones, Johanna, Castles to Cottages (2002)
- Medland, J.C., Shipwrecks of the Isle of Wight (1986)
- Mew, Fred, Back of the Wight (1957)
- Mitchell, Kevin, Newport Pubs (1999)
- Sprack, Gareth, At the Trail, Isle of Wight Rifles 1908 - 1920 (2014)
- Winter, C.W.R., The Manor Houses of the Isle of Wight (1984)

These books can be found in the Carisbrooke Castle Museum library collection, along with a wide range of other local history titles. The library is available to researchers by appointment.

Authors

Dr Rachel Tait is the Curator at Carisbrooke Castle Museum. She was born and brought up on the Isle of Wight before studying History of Art at the University of Bristol. Since returning to the Island, she has worked in a number of local museums, joining Carisbrooke Castle Museum in 2016. One of her main priorities for the museum's collection is acquiring contemporary artefacts, ensuring it remains relevant to future generations.

Kate Tiley is the Assistant Curator at Carisbrooke Castle Museum. She has lived in Carisbrooke for much of her life, spending time exploring the castle grounds as a child. Whilst studying History at the University of Chichester she volunteered at the museum and has been employed as a curatorial assistant since 2013. Her research interests include the museum's collection of historic costume and textiles.